The
LEEK and MANIFOLD
LIGHT RAILWAY

by
Stanley C. Jenkins, M.A.

Hulme End Station. Manifold Valley.

THE OAKWOOD PRESS

© S.C. Jenkins and Oakwood Press 1991

ISBN 0 85361 414 8

Typeset by Gem Publishing Company, Brightwell, Wallingford, Oxfordshire.

Printed and bound by Alpha Print, Crawley, Witney, Oxfordshire.

Wetton Mill Station, Manifold Valley, North Stafford Railway.

A three coach train at Wetton Mill as portrayed in a commercial postcard *c.*1905.
Oakwood Press Collection

Published by
The OAKWOOD PRESS
P.O.Box 122, Headington, Oxford.

Contents

A tranquil scene at Redhurst Crossing Halt with both passenger and staff gazing into the stream below, with no obvious speed to resume their journeys!

National Railway Museum

Introduction

The Leek & Manifold Valley Light Railway was one of Britain's lesser known narrow gauge railways. Built under the provisions of the Light Railways Act 1896, it was situated in a beautiful but remote part of Staffordshire that was slow to develop as a popular tourist area, and unlike many other narrow gauge lines, the Leek & Manifold had no lucrative quarry traffic to sustain it through the winter months. For these reasons the line relied primarily on local passenger traffic for its survival – the one busy time of the year being around July and August when excursionists flocked to the Manifold Valley area from their homes in neighbouring conurbations. Sadly, this locally-based summer tourist traffic fell away during the 1920s, and the railway was closed to all traffic on 10th March, 1934 – a victim of bus competition and neglect on the part of the LMS Railway that had inherited the line in 1923.

In 1937 the abandoned railway was re-opened as a scenic route for walkers, while in more recent years the route was partially converted into a motor road, its erstwhile stations becoming picnic areas for summer visitors. By a strange quirk of fate the Leek & Manifold Railway thereby gained a new lease of life as a modern tourist attraction, and paradoxically the route is better known today than at any time in its history!

This is by no means the first history of the Leek & Manifold Railway, but it is hoped that the present volume will throw at least some new light on aspects of the Leek & Manifold story. At the same time, an attempt has been made to provide a new collection of photographs that will not duplicate those found elsewhere. This book remained at the planning stage for several years – it being felt that *The Leek & Manifold Railway* should be included in the famous Oakwood range of light railway histories; it is hoped that the resulting volume will do much to keep the memory of the railway alive.

Stanley C. Jenkins
Witney, 1991

Footnotes and Sources

The present work is based entirely upon original sources, notably the Leek & Manifold Railway minute books and former Board of Trade documents held in the Public Record Office at Kew, and the collection of timetables, technical journals and official publications held by the University Library, Leicester. Secondary sources have not been consulted, to any great extent, though the author would like to give credit for material relating to the standard gauge Leek to Waterhouses line found in Basil Jeuda's *The Leek, Caldon & Waterhouses Railway* (Cheddleton 1980). It would be inappropriate to cite every source with extensive footnotes, but a limited number of source notes have nevertheless been included at the end of the book, primarily as a guide for further study.

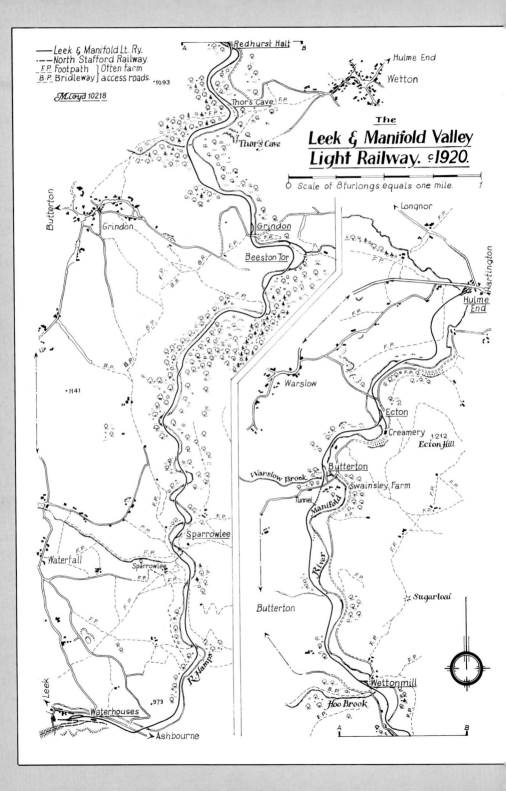

The
Leek & Manifold Valley
Light Railway. c.1920.

Scale of 8 furlongs equals one mile.

Leek & Manifold Lt. Ry.
North Stafford Railway.
F.P. Footpath } Often farm
B.P. Bridleway } access roads.

M.Loyd 10218

Historical Summary

Company of Origin:	Leek & Manifold Valley Light Railway
Light Railway Order:	Made on 6th March, 1899 when the construction of four railways was approved by the Light Railway Commissioners – Railway 1, Railway 2, Railway 3 to be built by the North Staffordshire Railway while Railway 4 would be the Leek & Manifold Valley Light Railway.
Capital:	Originally £15,000 in one pound shares, with free grant of £10,000 from HM Treasury and £10,000 in loans from Staffordshire County Council. A further £7,500 in loans and £7,500 by grant was made available by the Government prior to opening, while an extra £5,000 share capital had also been raised; an issue of £12,000 in debentures was authorised in 1911. By 1921 the accumulated debit balance was £14,000.
Directors (1899):	Charles Bill, Cheadle Staffs (MP for Leek and Honorary Colonel in the North Staffordshire Regiment).
	Sir Thomas Wardle, Swainsley Staffs (President of the Silk Association and noted amateur geologist).
	John P. Sheldon, Sheen Staffs (Professor of Agriculture at the Royal College of Agriculture, Cirencester).
	John Brealey, Leek Staffs (Leek Urban District Council).
	Andrew Moreton, Leek Staffs (Leek Urban District Council).
	A.J. Hambleton, Butterton Staffs (Leek Rural District Council).
	Frank Drewry, Buxton, Derbyshire.
	Alfred Hall, Waterhouses, Staffs.
	John Hall, Ball Haye Hall, Leek.
Gauge of Line:	2 ft 6 in. (with short sections of 4 ft 8½ in. gauge in sidings).
Date of Opening:	Monday 27th June, 1904 (ceremonial opening). Wednesday 29th June, 1904 (public goods and passenger services).
Length of Line:	Waterhouses to Hulme End 8¾ miles.
Mode of Operation:	Single line staff without intermediate passing places.
Locomotives:	Two 2−6−4 Kitson-built tank engines.
Rolling Stock:	Four coaches and eight freight vehicles.
Date of Closure:	Saturday 10th March, 1934.
Re-opened as Footpath:	Friday 23rd July, 1937.

TRAIN AT MOLLY'S END.
LEEK & MANIFOLD LIGHT RAILWAY

No. 1 2-6-4T (Kitson & Co. Ltd., Leeds.) ...offered at once and promised... *National Railway Museum*

Chapter One

Origins of the Line (1896–1905)

Staffordshire is seldom regarded as a mountainous area, and its scenery is sometimes dismissed as 'uninteresting'. It comes as a surprise, therefore, to discover that the north-eastern part of the county is a land of high moorland – an extension, in fact, of the well-known Peak District. Although this part of Staffordshire is highly scenic, it was, in Victorian times, a relatively little-known region with no rail links to the outside world. This was, in great part, an inevitable result of geography – after all, railways generally keep to the easiest terrain in order to keep construction costs within reasonable bounds. There were, nevertheless, a variety of railways on the edges of the Stafford-shire Peak, one of the earliest being the famous Cromford & High Peak line, which had originated in 1825 when its promoters obtained an Act (6th George IV cap. 30) providing consent for:

> Making and maintaining a railway or tramroad from the Cromford Canal, at or near Cromford, in the parish of Wirksworth, in the county of Derby, to the Peak Forest Canal, at or near Whaley . . . in the county of Chester.

The C&HPR was opened throughout by 1831, and in the next few years this pioneering line functioned successfully as an adjunct to the local canal system.[1]

Victorian Developments

The Cromford & High Peak Railway was primarily a freight line, but other local routes catered for both passenger and freight traffic. The Churnet Valley Railway, for example, ran from North Roade to Uttoxeter via Leek and Froghall, with a short 3 ft 6 in. gauge mineral branch to Caldon Low Quarries. Opened in 1849, the Churnet Valley route was part of the locally-based North Staffordshire Railway, whereas the neighbouring Cromford & High Peak line eventually passed into the open hands of the London & North Western Railway.

In 1852 a branch was opened from the NSR Churnet Valley line at Rocester to the Derbyshire town of Ashbourne, but otherwise a vast swathe of countryside between the Cromford & High Peak and Churnet Valley lines remained untouched by railways. This unsatisfactory situation remained unchanged until, in the 1890s, the LNWR opened a cross country route between Buxton and the existing North Staffordshire railhead at Ashbourne; this new line – which incorporated part of the much older Cromford & High Peak route – was opened between Buxton and Parsley Hay on 1st June, 1894, and completed throughout on 4th June, 1899.

The Buxton to Ashbourne line filled an important gap in the local transport system, but there was, as yet, no railway in the Manifold Valley area, and the inhabitants of scattered moorland settlements such as Warslow, Grindon and Hulme End had to rely on distant stations such as Leek, Cheddleton or Consol (all on the North Staffordshire Churnet Valley route) for their transport needs. Then, on 14th August, 1896 Parliament passed an Act for 'facilitating the construction of light railways' which would 'be found beneficial to the rural districts', and the new Act led to an upsurge in lightly-constructed railways serving rural areas.

The Light Railways Act of 1896

The Light Railway Act was the lineal descendent of a number of other Acts that had sought to simplify the system whereby railways could be built. The Railway Construction Facilities Act of 1864, for example, had enabled promoters to build lines in cases where all of the landowners concerned had agreed to the proposals. In Ireland, meanwhile, a series of Acts (such as the Relief & Distress Amendment Act of 1880) enabled railways to be constructed with financial help from local authorities, the idea being that such lines would help to erradicate rural poverty in Ireland's more distressed areas. Moreover, the promoters of these Irish lines were able to obtain an Order in Council from the Lord Lieutenant – an Act of Parliament being (in the majority of cases) unnecessary.[2]

The Light Railways Act of 1896 was similar to the various Irish Acts in that it enabled local and national government assistance to be made available to the promoters of light railways who (instead of obtaining an expensive Act of Parliament) would be able to apply for a much cheaper Light Railway Order. This system was facilitated by the creation of three Light Railway Commissioners, who were appointed by the Board of Trade to administer the scheme. The commissioners were given powers to grant Light Railway Orders in approved cases, although these Orders could, if necessary, be rejected by the Board of Trade. If local authorities agreed to subscribe to lines in their areas, the Treasury could provide loans of up to 25 per cent of the required capital, provided that 50 per cent of the capital was share capital subscribed for in the normal way.[3]

The new Act was warmly welcomed in the Manifold Valley district, and there were, in the 1890s, a number of proposals for the construction of light railways in this hitherto-railwayless region. Interestingly, some of these schemes actually predated the 1896 Act – there had, for instance, been talk of a tramway from Ashbourne to Derby, while the North Staffordshire Railway had itself considered the provision of narrow gauge lines as feeders to its main line system. These tentative proposals finally assumed tangible form when a group of local landowners and politicians persuaded the North Staffordshire Railway to support two light railways which, between them, would form a new route from Leek, on the existing Churnet Valley line, to Waterhouses, and thence via the Manifold Valley to a terminus at Hulme End.

First Steps

The idea that the Manifold Valley region might one day be connected to the outside world by a light railway was apparently first made in an address by the Reverend W. Beresford on 4th November, 1895, and his suggestion found ready support among members of the newly-created Leek Rural District Council.[4] There were initial thoughts of a link to the London &

North Western's proposed Buxton to Ashbourne line, but although such a scheme would have been welcomed by farmers and landowners in the Manifold and Hamps valley areas, the Leek councillors were keen to see a light railway link between Leek and the Manifold valley via the Dane valley. The Dane valley route would be longer and less convenient than a direct line to the LNWR at Buxton or Hartington, but it would be of great benefit to the town of Leek in that Manifold valley farmers would be encouraged to bring their produce to Leek (rather than rival marketing centres such as Ashbourne or Derby).

The Dane valley route was thus of great importance to Leek, and several public meetings were held in the town to discuss the proposed scheme. At the same time, the supporters of the Leek & Manifold line approached the North Staffordshire Railway in the hope that this important local company would be persuaded to back the Manifold valley project.

Amusingly, Mr W.S. Watson of the Leek Rural District Council had his own ideas of how the NSR might be encouraged to support the scheme. As *The Leek Post* recorded at the time, he 'judiciously invited the directors of the North Staffordshire Railway to a good luncheon at his house', and after the official party had feasted they were taken for a drive along the road to Waterhouses. With consumate guile, Mr Watson ensured that this outing took place on a market day , and it is said that the NSR Directors were greatly impressed by the endless stream of traffic that passed them on the road between Leek and Waterhouses! Needless to say, the North Staffordshire Board soon expressed interest in the scheme, and Mr Watson's informal approach was followed by further meetings and discussions between NSR representatives and a small committee of light railway supporters.[5]

It seemed that the hoped-for light railway was soon to become reality, but at the end of 1896 the promoters were alarmed to discover that other interests were planning a new main line from Derby to Manchester via Waterhouses and Leek. If implemented, this scheme would offer far better transport facilities than the proposed light railway, and for a time the light railway project remained in abeyance. In the event, the main line scheme was abandoned at an early date, and the light railway supporters and their North Staffordshire allies were able to continue with their own, more modest plans for a rail link between the NSR Churnet Valley route at Leek and the Manifold valley.

It was announced that the line would be promoted as the Leek, Caldon Low & Hartington Light Railways, and this new route would be constructed in two distinct sections, the western part, from Leek to Waterhouses, being a standard gauge line, while the eastern section would be a narrow gauge route. The standard gauge portion would be built by the North Staffordshire Railway, but the narrow gauge part would be constructed by a separate company and then worked, under terms to be agreed, by the NSR.

It was hoped that the proposed narrow gauge line from Waterhouses to Hulme End could be built for something in the region of £40,000, this modest sum being raised by share issue and by loans from national and local government sources under the provisions of the Light Railways Act. Meetings in support of the scheme were initially called in the name of 'The

Leek, Caldon Low & Hartington Light Railway', but it was soon decided that the narrow gauge line should be given an identity of its own, and on 21st September, 1898 the promoters of the Manifold Valley route held a committee meeting in the name of The Leek & Manifold Valley Light Railway.[6] This first L&MVLR meeting was a modest affair – the main item of business being the publication of a draft prospectus for the new company. It was agreed that 10,000 copies would be printed for circulation in the Manifold Valley area, and the promoters also agreed that 'the best paper should be used' for this important document.

The prospectus of 'The Leek & Manifold Valley Light Railway Company' was published in 1898, and those interested in the scheme were invited to apply for 15,000 one pound shares, the total share capital being £15,000. It was announced that the project was 'supported by a Free Grant of £10,000 from Her Majesty's Treasury and a loan of £10,000 from the Staffordshire County Council', while a further £20,000 could, if needed, be raised by loan.[7]

Supporters of the Scheme

The scheme was, from its inception, a locally-based project, and its leading supporters included several prominent local people. The most important promoters were perhaps Colonel Charles Bill, the Member of Parliament for the Leek Division of Staffordshire, and Sir Thomas Wardle of Swainsley Hall, near Hulme End. Charles Bill (1843–1915) was a well-known local landowner, while Sir Thomas Wardle (1831–1909) – whose wealth originated in the silk industry rather than land – had established himself as a country gentleman in the Manifold Valley area; both men clearly saw the proposed railway as a means of improvement for their tenants and for their own estates.

Other supporters of the Manifold scheme included John Brealey of Leek, Frank Drewry of Buxton, Alfred Hall of Waterhouses, John Hall of Leek, A.J. Hambleton of Leek, Andrew Moreton of Leek, and Professor J.P. Sheldon of Sheen, Staffordshire. A.J. Hambleton represented Leek Rural District Council while John Brealey and Andrew Moreton were both representatives of Leek Urban District Council; Professor Sheldon was similarly involved in local affairs, being Chairman of the Leek Board of Guardians. These nine gentlemen became the first Directors of the Leek & Manifold Valley Light Railway, while Colonel Bill – one of the most enthusiastic supporters of the L&MVLR scheme – was an ideal company Chairman.

The Leek & Manifold Valley Light Railway Secretary was Edward Challinor of Leek, and the company's bankers were the Manchester & Liverpool District Banking Company; the solicitors were Messrs Challinor & Shaw of Leek, and the Engineer was Joseph Forsyth of Fenton, Staffordshire. The company offices were at 10, Derby Street, Leek – the offices of Mr Challinor.

In theory, the promoters should have been well-placed to raise sufficient capital for the new railway. They were, after all, pillars of the local community who had subscribed their own money to the scheme as an example to their friends and neighbours! In the event the promoters experienced considerable difficulty in raising their £15,000 share capital, while some local residents objected to the proposed terminus at Hulme End which, as first planned, would have been sited near the centre of the village.

The Light Railway Order

Undeterred by these problems the promoters persisted with their scheme, an application for the necessary Light Railway Order being made in May 1897. The Light Railway Commissioners responded favourably to the scheme, and a Light Railway Order was made on 6th March, 1899.

The Order itself was a complex document providing consent, not only for the Leek & Manifold Railway but also for the connecting North Staffordshire Railway branch from Leek to Waterhouses. For convenience, the combined NSR–L&MVLR route was treated as four distinct railways, and these were defined as Railway No. 1, Railway No. 2, Railway No. 3 and Railway No. 4. Railways 1, 2 and 3 comprised the North Staffordshire line from Leek, together with a short branch to Caldon Quarries, while Railway No. 4 was the Leek & Manifold Valley line. The latter was carefully defined as a railway:

> 8 miles 8 chains or thereabouts in length commencing in the . . . parish of Caldon at the termination of Railway No. 3 and terminating in the parish of Warslow and Ecton in the field numbered 508 on the 1-2500 Ordnance Map of that parish.[8]

The order stipulated that Railways 1, 2 and 3 would be 4 ft 8½ in. gauge lines, but Railway 4 would, in contrast, 'be constructed on a gauge of 2 feet 6 inches'. There was a time limit of three years for the compulsory purchase of land, and five years were allowed for completion of the works. Other clauses dealt with the tolls to be charged on the new railways and in this context it is interesting to record that the tolls on Railways 1, 2 and 3 would be the same as those applicable to a main line; overall speed limits of 25 miles per hour would apply on Railways 1, 2 and 3, but the Leek & Manifold section would be subject to an even stricter speed limit of 15 miles per hour. Further clauses dealt with technical matters such as the weight of rail to be laid on the Leek & Manifold line (35 lb. per yard) and the provision of level crossings.[9]

Having obtained their Order the promoters – now organised as a proper Board of Directors – were understandably keen to begin work on the line, and the first sod was ceremonially cut at Waterhouses on 3rd October, 1899. There was, however, no attempt to commence work on the major earthworks, and the scheme suffered an unexpected blow at the end of the year when Mr Forsyth, the Engineer, died.

The company had, in the meantime, employed another engineer – Mr E.R. Calthrop – as a consultant, and he had already suggested ways in which the line might be improved. It seemed that Mr Calthrop would be the ideal replacement for Mr Forsyth, and he was accordingly appointed as Engineer to the Leek & Manifold Valley Light Railway Company.

In retrospect, the appearance of Everard Calthrop can be seen as something of a turning point in Leek & Manifold affairs. The company's financial position remained precarious, but in Mr Calthrop the L&MVLR had an

Engineer of strong opinions and sound experience. He had recently put some of his many ideas into practice on the Barsi Light Railway. This 2 ft 6 in. gauge Indian line crossed the Bombay to Raichur main line of the Great Indian Peninsula Railway at Kurduwadi, and its first section had been opened to traffic in 1897. The Barsi line was built to very strict standards in an attempt to ensure a uniform axle loading of 5 tons per axle; its track and bridges were cheaply but adequately constructed, while locomotives, rolling stock and other details owed much to Mr Calthrop's own designs. Having initiated his system in India, Mr Calthrop was eager to implement his ideas in the United Kingdom, and it comes as no surprise to discover that many features of the line were faithfully copied on the Leek & Manifold Railway.

The Calthrop System

In planning the Leek & Manifold Railway Mr Calthrop and his assistants were determined that a series of principles would be strictly applied, and for this reason it could be said that the L&MVLR was built on the 'Calthrop System'. The system had been partially implemented on the Barsi line, but certain important features of the L&MVLR were based upon entirely new concepts that (as far as can be ascertained) had never been tested on any other railway. It would, therefore, be useful to examine the so-called Calthrop System in greater detail before describing how these novel ideas were put into practice on the Manifold line.

In essence, the pivotal feature of Calthrop's plan was the employment of a uniform axle load of only 5 tons; this lightweight loading would reduce wear and tear on the track, thereby allowing the track itself to be built as cheaply as possible. It was envisaged that the Manifold line would be laid with flat-bottomed rails weighing only 35 lb. per yard, this figure being in marked contrast to the much heavier 50 lb. or 68 lb. rails used by contemporary narrow gauge lines such as the Vale of Rheidol or Cork Blackrock & Passage railways (see Appendix 3).

Although the Leek & Manifold trackwork would be of the cheapest possible type, the Calthrop System anticipated that rolling stock would be built to the very limits of the loading gauge as a means of ensuring maximum carrying capacity. Bogie stock was preferred and, with adequate clearance over bridges and through tunnels, Mr Calthrop envisaged that the L&MVLR passenger vehicles would be almost as large as contemporary main line coaches. Moreover, having designed the line to accommodate outsize coaching stock, it would be possible to run *standard gauge* vehicles over the new railway by making use of novel 'transporter cars'.

The transporter (or 'transportation' cars) were one of the most interesting features of the Calthrop System. Such vehicles had been planned for use on the Barsi line but none had been delivered – indeed the project was still, in 1899, at the experimental stage. It was nevertheless intended that the Leek & Manifold line would be able to carry standard gauge vehicles, and that 4 ft 8½ in. gauge stock would be speedily and easily transferred to and from short lengths of standard gauge track at each L&MVLR goods yard.

The Calthrop System incorporated a number of other innovations of various kinds, including the use of Jones-Calthrop centre buffer/couplings and a range of minor locomotive improvements that had been devised by the Engineer. Some of these ideas were no doubt costly, but having saved considerable sums in terms of trackwork Mr Calthrop may have felt justified in spending more money on other items. He was, furthermore, a persuasive character who seems to have had no difficulty in imposing his will on the pliant and inexperienced Leek & Manifold Directors. There was also the very real possibility that any excessive expenditure could be blamed on supposed 'miscalculations' made by the late Mr Forsyth – and L&MVLR records show that the unfortunate Mr Forsyth was conveniently blamed for a variety of mistaken calculations.

An early colour postcard published in 1905 by Alpha Ltd of the line near Beeston Tor. The card showed both engine and coaches in a pale crimson.   *Oakwood Collection*

The opening day on 27th June, 1904 with the two locomotives hauling a well overloaded train. Note the people standing on both engines

Chapter Two

Construction and Opening (1900–1905)

Construction of the 8¾ mile long narrow gauge railway commenced in March 1902, the resident Engineer being John Earle while the principal contractors were Messrs Hutchinson & Co. This same firm had already secured the contracts for Railways 1, 2 and 3, but the Leek & Manifold Directors were reluctant to accept their tender for Railway No. 4 because the contractors refused to reduce their quote below £44,000. After some argument the L&MVLR bowed to North Staffordshire pressure and accepted Mr Hutchinson's tender; however, Hutchinsons then sublet the contract to Messrs Lovatt & Co. of Wolverhampton, and in practice this latter firm carried out much of the work on the new line.

Preliminaries to Construction

Overall control of the project was entrusted to Mr Calthrop, and this somewhat forceful character acted as a very able intermediary in dealings with North Staffordshire officers such as W.D. Phillipps – the company's General Manager. In carrying out the work Mr Calthrop was assisted by John Earle and Mr E. Godfrey Brewer. John Earle was very closely involved in the project, being frequently on site during the period of construction, but Mr Godfrey Brewer – whose sphere of interest was mechanical engineering – seems to have spent most of his time in London, where he collaborated closely with Everard Calthrop in drawing up plans and specifications for the locomotives and rolling stock.

It was necessary, before construction could begin, for the Leek & Manifold Directors to liaise with neighbouring landowners in order that the requisite land could be obtained on mutually-agreeable terms. This process was, inevitably, a long and frustrating one involving a variety of private agreements between the railway company and the landowners concerned. Ironically, one of the most 'difficult' property owners was Sir Thomas Wardle, who jealously guarded his privacy at Swainsley Hall (near Butterton). A series of complex negotiations ensued, this thorny matter being more than usually sensitive because Sir Thomas was, in all other respects, a committed supporter of the whole scheme. In the end, a compromise route was finally agreed – albeit at greater expense than would otherwise have been necessary.

In contrast to Sir Thomas Wardle, Earl Cathcart welcomed the railway, though his request for a siding at Beeston Tor did not entirely please the L&MVLR Directors; elsewhere, local landowners and their tenants needed various means of access from one side of the line to the other, their demands being satisfied by the provision of occupation crossings at suitable locations. (Such crossings cost little to install, and in this respect the promoters were fortunate that, as the owners of a light railway, they were unlikely to be called upon to build expensive over or underbridges merely to allow cattle to pass across the line.)

The projected route commenced in the Hamps Valley at Waterhouses and then followed the Hamps Valley downstream to Beeston Tor where (in wet

NORTH STAFFORDSHIRE RAILWAY.

THE MANIFOLD VALLEY LIGHT RAILWAY

WILL BE OPENED FOR TRAFFIC

On Wednesday, June 29th, 1904

Train Service: Week Days only.

Miles			First and Third Class only						Fares Third Class	Miles			First and Third Class only						Fares Third Class
from Leek			a.m.	a.m.	p.m.	p.m.	p.m.		from Leek	from Hulme End			a.m.	a.m.	p.m.	p.m.	p.m.		from Hulme End
8	Leek (Railway station)	dep	8 50	11 15	2 15	5 0	7 25											•	Single / Return
	by Motor Omnibus					•	x			1	Hulme End (for Hartington)	dep	9 5	11 35	2 30	5 10	7 40		
	Waterhouses	arr	9 50	12 15	3 15	6 0	8 25	8d.	1	Ecton (for Warslow)		9 10	11 40	2 35	5 16	7 45	1d.	2d.
Miles from Waterhouses									from Waterhouses Single / Return	2	Butterton		9 13	11 43	2 38	5 20	7 48	2d.	3d.
	Waterhouses	dep	10 5	12 30	3 30	6 15	8 40		3	Wetton Mill		9 19	11 49	2 44	5 27	7 54	3d.	5d.
2	Sparrowlee		10 15	12 38	3 38	6 23	8 48	2d.	3d.	4	Thor's Cave		9 25	11 55	2 49	5 32	7 59	4d.	6d.
4	Beeston Tor		10 25	12 48	3 45	6 34	8 58	4d.	7d.	5	Grindon		9 29	11 59	2 54	5 38	8 4	5d.	8d.
4	Grindon		10 28	12 51	3 51	6 37	9 1	4d.	7d.	6	Beeston Tor		9 32	12 2	2 57	5 41	8 7	5d.	8d.
5	Thor's Cave		10 31	12 58	3 56	6 45	9 6	5d.	8d.	7	Sparrowlee		9 42	12 13	3 7	5 52	8 17	7d.	1/-
6	Wetton Mill		10 36	1 4	4 1	6 48	9 11	6d.	10d.	9	Waterhouses	arr	9 50	12 20	3 15	6 0	8 25	8d.	1/1
7	Butterton		10 42	1 7	4 7	6 55	9 17	7d.	1/-	from Waterhouses									from Waterhouses
8	Ecton (for Warslow)		10 45	1 10	4 10	6 59	9 20	8d.	1/1		Waterhouses	dep	10 5	12 35		6	8 40	
9	Hulme End (for Hartington)	arr	10 50	1 15	4 15	7 5	9 25	9d.	1/3		by Motor Omnibus								
										8	Leek (Railway Station)	arr	11 5	1 35		7	8 40	8d.

* Thursdays and Saturdays only, Motor Omnibus and Train.　　　　x Thursdays and Saturdays excepted. Motor Omnibus only.

N.B.—The Motor Omnibus will carry 22 Passengers, and only that number will be accepted for conveyance; and in all cases preference will be given to Passengers arriving or going forward by Railway.

MARKET TICKETS

will be issued to **LEEK** on WEDNESDAYS and SATURDAYS at Reduced Fares, viz.:

From Hulme End 1s.6d., all other Stations 1s.3d., Third Class.

LUGGAGE.—Holders of Market Tickets are permitted to carry Baskets or other Packages containing Eggs, Butter, Fruit, or other Market Produce of their own Rearing, not exceeding 28 lbs. in weight, without charge. Packages exceeding 28 lbs. in weight will be charged at ordinary Parcels Rates; but notice that they are not and will not be responsible for any article so conveyed by Passengers. If required to be conveyed at the Company's risk, ordinary Rates will be charged.

On MONDAYS, THURSDAYS and SATURDAYS, Cheap Excursion Tickets will be issued at STOKE Station to Hulme End or any intermediate Station.

Fare 3/- for the Double Journey.

Important Notice to Cyclists.

Free Storage (at the owner's risk) will be provided for the day at Waterhouses, for the Cycles of parties arriving there by road and proceeding by rail to any Station on the Manifold Valley Railway.

Scale of Parcels Rates.

Parcels between Leek and Waterhouses or Hulme End and intermediate points will be charged as follows:—

Not exceeding	- - -	10 lbs.	6d. each.
Above 10 and not exceeding	20 „	8d. „
„ 20 „ „	28 „	10d. „

Parcels weighing above 28 lbs. will not be accepted for conveyance on the Railway.

LUGGAGE.—Ordinary Passengers are allowed to carry 40lbs. weight free all being personal luggage and not goods, merchandise, or other articles carried for sale, hire or profit.

W. D. PHILLIPPS, General Manager.

The timetable poster issued for the opening of the Railway on 29th June, 1904.

Oakwood Collection

weather) the Hamps joined forces with the River Manifold. Turning north-
westwards the route continued along the Manifold Valley via Grindon,
Wetton and Ecton to a terminus at Hulme End.

At Ecton, the proposed route traversed an area of abandoned lead and
copper mines. In their 18th century heyday these once-extensive workings
had yielded vast profits for the Duke of Devonshire – who was thereby able
to finance the building of grandiose projects such as the famous Crescent at
Buxton. Foreign competition eventually forced the Ecton mines to close, but
the spoil heaps left by the 18th century miners were of obvious use to the
railway builders, and having arranged for a crusher to be erected on the site
the L&MVLR Directors were able to purchase an unlimited supply of stone
and gravel at three farthings per ton. This waste material was of immense
help during the construction of the Manifold line and, as an added bonus,
any surplus stone could be sold, at considerable profit, to neighbouring
farmers.[10]

With construction at last underway the Directors were able to give at least
some consideration to the question of locomotives and rolling stock, but in
practice the major decisions in these matters were left in the able hands of
Mr Calthrop.

Choice of Rolling Stock

The type of passenger rolling stock that would be needed to work the line
was a matter of some controversy and, not for the first time, there were
pronounced differences of opinion between, on the one hand, the North
Staffordshire Railway, and on the other the firm-minded Mr Calthrop. The
NSR General Manager had envisaged that the future Leek & Manifold
Railway would be worked by coaches with conventional side doors, but Mr
Calthrop disagreed and he proposed instead a small fleet of American-type
bogie saloons.

It was perhaps, only natural that the L&MVLR Engineer should have
advocated saloon-type vehicles; his experience in India had demonstrated
that rolling stock of this type was perfectly adequate in everyday service,
whereas Mr Phillipps would clearly have been more familiar with the small,
compartment-type carriages used in England at that time. To his credit, the
NSR General Manager tactfully bowed to Mr Calthrop's greater experience in
these matters, and what might have developed into a major row was defused
at an early date. Having won the argument vis-à-vis rolling stock design Mr
Calthrop was free to implement the 'Calthrop System' without hindrance,
and on 7th May, 1902 he arrived at a Leek & Manifold Directors' meeting
armed with a set of plans for the new vehicles. The L&MVLR minute book
records that:

> The sketch plans of the passenger carriages for first and third class only were fully
> gone into and explained by Mr Calthrop, and he reported that Mr Phillipps had
> seen and approved the sketch plans as produced, and it was resolved that the same
> be approved with the exception that arms at the sides of the seats be dispensed
> with.[11]

The question of lighting was left unresolved, and the minute book does not record what, if any, discussion took place on this topic. Reading 'between the lines', it is conceivable that Mr Calthrop wanted electric lighting, whereas the Directors (thinking perhaps of the cost of this luxury feature) may have preferred oil lamps. If this supposition is correct Mr Calthrop must have won another argument because the four coaches, when eventually delivered, were equipped with Stone's Patent Electric Lighting System. (In fact, Mr Calthrop's will prevailed in every difference of opinion that ever arose between him and his employers – the coaches were, for instance, finally built *with* arm rests, even though the Directors had decided against them!)

A further question arose at the Directors' meeting held at Leek on 21st May, 1902, when there was some thought of asking for a combined tender for locomotives and rolling stock. This idea had superficial attractions, but as most railway engineering firms specialised in locomotive construction, carriage building or signalling, it was resolved 'that separate tenders be asked for the locomotives and carriages, and that it be left to the Engineer to decide as to the selection of the firms who should be asked to tender'.[12]

In the event, five locomotive building firms submitted tenders for the construction of two engines,· the most promising tender being that from Bagnalls who quoted just £1,450 per engine. Other quotations ranged from £1,560 from Beyer Peacock of Manchester, to £1,975 from the North British Locomotive Company, but the company seemed content to accept a tender of £1,725 from Kitsons of Leeds on the recommendation of their Engineer. It will be noted that Kitson's quotation was by no means the cheapest, but the Leeds firm had already built a batch of 0–8–4Ts to Calthrop's design for the Barsi Light Railway, and perhaps for this reason the L&MVLR Engineer was keen for Kitson's to build the Manifold Valley engines.

Planning the Stations

The new line was well advanced by the early months of 1904, and with the cuttings and other earthworks substantially complete the Directors turned their thoughts to the provision of intermediate stations on the 8¾ mile single line. These were to be little more than halts, with waiting shelters for passengers, but with no provisions for station staff – tickets would instead be issued on the trains. It was agreed that Beeston Tor and Thor's Cave stations would be provided with refreshment rooms, while Hulme End would be a much more substantial station with an engine shed, covered accommodation for carriages, and full booking facilities; most of the L&MVLR's buildings were supplied by the Portable Building Company of Fleetwood, but the engine and carriage sheds were erected by Isaac Dixon & Company.[13]

The L&MVLR minute book provides much useful information about the planning and equipment of the Leek & Manifold stations. On 9th March, 1904, for example, the Directors agreed that simple waiting shelters would be obtained from the Portable Building Company at the price of £40 each, while a somewhat larger structure from the same firm would be erected at

Hulme End for £137 11s. It was also agreed that Isaac Dixon & Co's tender of £219 for the engine shed at Hulme End was acceptable, though the price of the carriage shed was higher at £258.

Smaller items for use at the stations included a set of twelve station seats at 18s. 6d. each and (at another meeting) the Directors discussed the possibility of obtaining pumping equipment for the water supply at Hulme End from Merryweathers – the famous London-based fire engine manufacturers. It was suggested that, when delivered, the platform seats should be adorned with the name of each station in shaded letters, (photographs confirm that the names were applied).

Other matters discussed during the early months of 1904 included the station names, one decision being that the stopping place to be provided at Weag's Bridge would be called 'Grindon', while Swainsley station would be known as 'Butterton'. A year earlier, in April 1903, the L&MVLR Directors had decided that 'there was no need for a crossing station at Weag's Bridge', but if the North Staffordshire Railway insisted on one 'it would be advisable' to put the loop at Wetton Mill.[14] Implicit in this decision was the assumption that the Manifold line would be worked as simply as possible on the 'one-engine-in-steam' system without intermediate passing places on the 8¾ mile single line.

There were fears that the NSR (which, as the operating company would have a say in these matters) would require expensive signalling systems, but happily there was no dispute on this matter. On the other hand the North Staffordshire company was not afraid to demand certain other pieces of equipment that the Leek & Manifold Directors would not otherwise have supplied. The NSR was insistent, for example, that a Pooley weighing machine should be installed at Hulme End, and a weigh-bridge was accordingly built behind the new wooden station building at the L&MVLR's upper terminus.

Other equipment needed for the Manifold line included a basic telephone system for communication between the upper and lower termini, and a rudimentary signalling system at Waterhouses and Hulme End. It was eventually agreed that the telephone would be supplied by the North Staffordshire Railway's own Electrical Engineer, while signalling equipment would be supplied by the specialist signalling firm of McKenzie & Holland.

Last Minute Problems

The first locomotives were probably at work on the unfinished line by 1902 or 1903, and in this context it is interesting to discover that at least two contractors engines were employed on the Leek & Manifold contract. The engines concerned were called *Skylark* and *Sirdar* (the Indian connotations of the latter being significant in view of E.R. Calthrop's association with the Barsi Light Railway). Unfortunately, the two Kitson engines were delivered later than anticipated, and although the Directors had announced that the line would be opened for public traffic on Whit Monday 1904 (23rd May) the railway was not ready for opening until the following June. Amusingly, a

London newspaper announced that the railway *had* opened on 23rd May – an account which (as *The Railway Magazine* remarked) could 'not . . . be commended for its accuracy'!

It had, in the meantime, been agreed that the Leek & Manifold Valley Light Railway would be worked by the North Staffordshire company for a period of 99 years in return for 55 per cent of the gross annual receipts; the remaining 45 per cent would be available for dividends after interest and other charges had been met – though it was nevertheless anticipated that a small dividend would indeed be paid.

Costs had, by 1904, exceeded the estimates 'very considerably', and it was, in consequence, necessary to increase the company's share capital from £15,000 to £20,000. Further help had also been provided by the government, the original free grant of £10,000 being increased to £17,500 while, at the same time, the government granted an additional £7,500 by loan. The total capital available at the time of opening was as shown below:

Original share capital	£15,000
Additional share capital	£5,000
Government grants	£17,500
Government loans	£7,500
Staffordshire County Council loan	£10,000
Total cost	£55,000

The county council was to be repaid at 3½·per cent per annum within a period of 50 years, and the government loan was repayable at 3 per cent. If, by any chance, the company was unable to repay the local authority loan, the county council was empowered to raise the money by means of rates to be levied in villages served by the new railway.

Mr Everard R. Calthrop, M.I.C.E.,
Chief Mechanical Engineer.

Mr John B. Earle, *Resident Engineer.*

The Locomotives Arrive

A further problem presented itself in 1904 when it was realised that the connecting NSR branch line between Leek and Waterhouses could not be ready for opening until the following year. The contractors had fallen behind with the work, and, as usual in such situations, there was more than a hint of ill-feeling between Messrs Hutchinson and the North Staffordshire Railway.

A more immediate problem, as far as the Leek & Manifold Railway was concerned, was the method by which two heavy locomotives and several items of rolling stock could be transported to Waterhouses in the absence of a proper rail link. The L&MVLR minute book does not indicate how this problem was finally solved, although there was some talk about the extra cost of delivery. It was possible for locomotives to be mounted on temporary wheels and pulled across country by teams of horses, but on reflection it is more likely that the two Leek & Manifold engines were delivered over the unfinished NSR branch. The standard gauge line would have been sufficiently complete for the passage of engineering trains, and one assumes that the L&MVLR equipment was delivered in conventional standard gauge rolling stock; both engines were certainly installed on the line by April 1904.

The Board of Trade Inspection

It was necessary, before the line was opened for public traffic, for the newly-completed narrow gauge line to be thoroughly inspected by a Board of Trade Inspector, and in the early summer of 1904 the NSR and L&MVLR companies were informed that the inspection would be carried out by Major F. Druitt on behalf of the BoT.

Major Druitt traversed the line in the following June, and having inspected the new works the Inspector jotted down a very full description of the track, stations and engineering features. His report, dated 23rd June, 1904, is worth examining in detail insofar as it furnishes us with an expert, eye-witness account of the Leek & Manifold Light Railway at the very start of its operational life.[15] As usual, the Inspector commenced his report with an elegant introduction and then immediately launched into a detailed technical description:

Sir,

I have the honour to report, for the information of the Board of Trade, that in compliance with the instructions contained in your minute . . . . I have inspected the Leek & Manifold Lt. Railway, or Railway No. 4 of the Leek, Caldon and Hartington Lt. Railway Order 1898.

This light railway of 2 ft 6 in. gauge commences at Hulme End in the parish of Warslow and terminates at Waterhouses in the parish of Caldon. It is 8 miles in length.

It is a single line and no land has been purchased for widening. The width of the formation level is 10 ft on embankments and 12 ft to 15 ft in cuttings.

The sharpest curve has a radius of 4 chains and the steepest gradient an inclination of 1 in 50. The deepest cutting has a depth of 15 ft and the highest embankment of 17 ft.

Both engines at Hulme End awaiting in steam for duty   *National Railway Museum*

The permanent way consists of Vignoles steel rail weighing 35 pounds per yard, 24 ft in length, fastened to creosoted fir sleepers 5 ft × 8 in. × 4 in. by spikes and screws, rail bearing plates being also provided. The fishplates weigh 12½ lbs. per yard and are 16 in. in length, and the rails are fastened thereto by 4 × ⅝ in. bolts and nuts.

The bottom ballast is stated to be of hard packed stone 6 inches in depth, and the top is of broken stone.

The line is fenced throughout consisting of post and rail, top rail 4 ft above ground, or of wire fencing, top strand 3 ft 10 in. above ground, or of dry stone walling 4 ft above ground. The drainage is of the ordinary description.

There are 24 underbridges, ten of which have two spans each. Eighteen of the bridges are formed of plate girders and cross sleepers fastened to them, five are of rolled joists and one of timber beams under each rail, and all have masonry abutments. The largest span, on the skew, is 40 ft.

There are 3 culverts of more than 3 ft diameter, all of suitable construction. All the bridges have a very substantial appearance and are standing well.

The Inspector then noted that Waterhouses station 'would not be used at present for passenger traffic', and for this reason about ¼ mile of track at the southern end of the line would not be brought into use for public traffic until later. Making no objection to this course of action, he reported that there were 'ground platforms' at Sparrowlee, Beeston Tor, Grindon, Thor's Cave, Wetton Mill, Butterton, Ecton and Hulme End:

Sidings, some worked by a single lever ground frame controlled by the train staff, have been provided at Sparrowlee, Grindon, Wetton Mill and Ecton. At Hulme End there are two siding connections and a run-round road for the engines worked from a ground frame of 5 levers. This frame is at present controlled by a special key proposed to be kept by the station master, but this is to be abolished and the ground frame controlled by the train staff only.

There are six public road level crossings at one of which, viz. the Leek & Ashbourne turnpike, gates have been provided, and a gatekeeper is to be in attendance. At the others cattle guards have been provided. Speed across the five is restricted to 10 miles an hour by Clause 33(3) of the Order and special boards are required to be erected at points 300 yards on either side of them as directed by Clause 26(b) of the Order . . . the line is worked by one engine in steam (or two coupled together) . . . The rolling stock and the centre buffer couplings seem very suitable. The permanent way is in excellent order, and subject to the above requirements and to the provision of lighting arrangements before the winter (which the Company are going to provide on the platforms) I can recommend the Board of Trade to sanction the use of the above line for passenger traffic.

I have, etc.,

F. Druitt,
Major R.E.

In general, the Inspector was very pleased with what he had seen during his visit, and the use of phrases such as 'substantial appearance', 'very suitable' and 'excellent order' underlined the fact that the new line had passed its first test with flying colours!

A further view on opening day when the two low-sided bogie wagons were used to carry the numerous guests on the first public run.

Oakwood Collection

Opening of the Line

Having passed its Board of Trade inspection the Leek & Manifold line was ceremonially opened on Monday 27th June, 1904. As usual on such occasions the Great Day was celebrated in style, with flags, speeches and a grand luncheon for the specially-invited guests. On a controversial note, the Directors and shareholders were expected to pay for their tickets, and a suggestion that local schoolchildren might be given a free trip on one of the first trains was abruptly dismissed. Happily, Opening Day was bright and sunny, and all the participants agreed that the event was a great success.

The proceedings began at Waterhouses when the new railway was formally declared open by the Lord Lieutenant of Staffordshire. At 11.23 am the Directors and their guests boarded a double-headed special train consisting of two bright yellow coaches and two open wagons fitted with seats, and after a return trip to Hulme End the official party proceeded to a large marquee that had been erected in a field near the Post Office. Here, a lunch had been prepared for several hundred guests, and at the conclusion of the meal the diners listened to speeches made by Sir Thomas Wardle, Charles Bill, the Earl of Dartmouth and other speakers. Meanwhile, the railway was opened to the general public, and large numbers of first-day travellers were able to enjoy a celebratory ride over the new line to Hulme End.

The first day celebrations were fully reported in the local press, and also by *The Railway Magazine* which subsequently printed a very full description of the new line, together with an interesting eye-witness account of the opening ceremony:

The opening ceremony was performed by the Earl of Dartmouth, Lord Lieutenant of the county of Stafford, in the presence of the Chairman of the Board, most of the Directors, and many leading officials connected with railways in this country and abroad. In addition, there was a large gathering of gentlemen of local influence and of the inhabitants of the district generally.

The arrangements were admirably carried out under the direction of Mr E. Challinor, the Secretary of the Board, the value of whose services in connection with the undertaking from its inception was referred to in most favourable terms by the Chairman and other speeches at the luncheon . . . on arrival at Waterhouses we found the little town en fête, gay with flags and banners, and arches of evergreens, while mottoes, more or less appropriate, were displayed at intervals. One, 'Hurry up, North Stafford', was evidently intended as a reminder to the North Staffordshire Railway to get its connecting branch complete as soon as possible. This work is being pushed forwards rapidly, and pending its completion the North Staffordshire Railway is running motor carriages from Leek to Waterhouses and from the Manifold Valley. Unfortunately, one of these cars broke down on the day of opening, the passengers having to complete their journey in wagonettes.

At the terminus of the light railway we found a train consisting of two carriages and two trucks provided with temporary seats. Lord Dartmouth having briefly declared the line open, the invited guests took their seats, and we started on what proved to be an exceedingly pleasant journey.

The River Manifold (sometimes Manyfold) is said to take its name from its many windings or folds, and the Hamps is not far behind in this respect. Both streams are remarkable from the fact that they disappear underground at a point about 2 miles distant from each other, and reappear as one river some 3 miles farther down, near Ilam Church.

We accomplished the run of 8½ miles in 34 minutes, not an excessive speed, but sufficient for those who wished to enjoy the glorious scenery – now viewed by most of us for the first time – through which we passed. On the day before our visit the engine took the train the entire distance at the rate of 30 miles an hour.

Including those at Hulme End and Waterhouses, there are seven stations on the line. Each has a good platform and a capacious wooden building, called by the railway company a bungalow, for the shelter and refreshment of excursion and picnic parties. Booking offices are not required as the tickets are issued and collected in the train.

At Hulme End there is quite a respectable station, with capacious sheds for goods and engines and coaching stock. Here a short stay was made whilst Mr Brewer explained the working of the transport car, and the visitors inspected the line and station. The transport car was attached to the train, and we returned to Waterhouses at a rather higher speed than we made on the outward journey.

At Waterhouses luncheon was spread in a large marquee, and several hundred people, their appetites sharpened by the bracing air of the hills, heartily partook thereof. Congratulatory speeches were made by the Earl of Dartmouth, Mr Charles Bill MP, Sir Thomas Wardle, Colonel Boughey, a member of the Light Railway Commission, and other gentlemen.[16]

The *Railway Magazine* report noted that the district traversed by the railway was 'very thinly populated', the nature of the land being so difficult and irregular that 'the expense of an ordinary line would have been prohibitive'. It was hoped that there were 'resources amongst the hills and dales' that could be developed now that the Leek & Manifold Railway was in operation, a revival of mining activities at Ecton being just one of the many advantages that were expected to accrue from the new line. On a more modest scale it was also hoped that farmers would send 'milk and butter and cheese to the large towns in the Potteries, or to more distant Liverpool and Manchester', while, in the opposite direction, it was anticipated that a large tourist and holiday traffic would be attracted during the summer months.

Regular services commenced on Wednesday 29th June, 1904, with an initial train service of three up and three down trains between Hulme End and Waterhouses. There were departures from Hulme End at 9.05, 11.35 am and 5.10 pm, while balancing northbound workings left Waterhouses at 10.05 am, 12.30 and 6.15 pm. Additional trains ran on Thursdays and Saturdays only, and these extra services left Hulme End at 2.30 and 7.40 pm, with corresponding return workings from Waterhouses at 3.30 and 8.30 pm respectively.

The average journey time was 40–45 minutes for the 8½ mile journey, and the third class single fare from Waterhouses to Hulme End was 9d. Ordinary third class returns tickets were available for 1s. 3d. in each direction, and through bookings were advertised to and from Leek; however, as the North Staffordshire branch between Waterhouses and Leek was not yet in operation potential through travellers were conveyed beyond Waterhouses in NSR steam buses (which were, somewhat confusingly, referred to as 'motor buses').

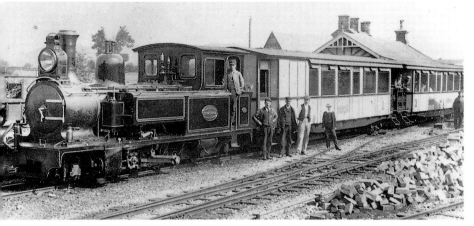

Another early view of Hulme End, *c.*1904. A brand new *E.R. Calthrop* poses for the camera; even at this early date the engine is running with the bunker towards Hulme End. *Lens of Sutton*

No. 2 *J.B. Earle* stands in the platform at Hulme End shortly after the line's opening. The standard gauge siding in the foreground was laid with 35 lb. rail. *Lens of Sutton*

Below Locomotive No. 2 *J.B. Earle* pauses on one of the line's many underbridges with a single coach train. The presence of two ladies on the footplate suggests a test train – perhaps in the days preceding public opening in June 1904. *L.&.G.R.P. Collection*

Some Details of the Line

The newly-opened 2 ft 6 in. gauge line was substantially-built and, in order to accommodate standard gauge wagons on Everard Calthrop's distinctive transporter wagons its loading gauge was equivalent to that of a standard gauge branch. The tunnel at Swainsley, for example, was 15¼ ft high and 12 ft wide, while the Leek & Manifold Valley rolling stock was much larger than any previously constructed for an English narrow gauge line. Indeed, the L&MVLR coaches were so spacious that an admiring *Railway Magazine* correspondent thought that 'when looking at one of these carriages' one could 'scarcely realise' that they were running on a 2 ft 6 in. gauge line! These sentiments were echoed by *The Locomotive Magazine* which, on 15th July, 1904, described the new vehicles as follows:

> This rolling stock would appear to be of an abnormal size for a railway of only 2 ft 6 in. gauge, but experience in India and the West Indies has proved after seven year's work that it is absolutely safe. Whatever doubts anyone may have as to the stability of these coaches can be immediately dispelled by riding in them; they travel most smoothly, without any vibration or roll. Before the opening ceremony these coaches were tested at a speed of 30 miles per hour over the entire railway. The speed at which they will run when the line is open to the public is only 12 miles an hour.
>
> The coaches are 42 ft long over headstocks, 8 ft wide overall, 6 ft 9 in. wide inside, and 10t high from rail level to top of roof, giving 6 ft 6 in. headroom at the lowest point inside. It will be noted that these dimensions are very little less than the dimensions of a modern main line vehicle, and are far greater than those of a large number of coaches still in use on standard gauge railways in this country. The coaches are of two types, namely composite 1st, 3rd and guard's compartment, and 3rd class only. The composites are provided with seats for 22 third class passengers and eight first class. The 3rd class coaches have seating accommodation for 44 passengers . . . Stone's patent system of electric lighting is fitted, and all the rolling stock is fitted with the automatic vacuum brake. The passenger coaches were built by the Electric Railway and Tramway Carriage Works Ltd., of Preston.[17]

Four coaches had been ordered from the Electric Railway & Tramway Works, but only two arrived in time for the public opening in June 1904, and for this reason the 'First Train' included two goods wagons in its formation. The remaining two vehicles were delivered a few weeks later, the four coaches being numbered in sequence from 1 to 4. The locomotives, meanwhile, had been numbered 1 and 2, and given the names *E.R. Calthrop* and *J.B. Earle* respectively. Two open wagons and two transporter vehicles were also available at the time of opening, other rolling stock being delivered later (*see Chapter Five*).

There were originally seven intermediate stopping places between Waterhouses and Hulme End, most of these tiny stations being equipped with facilities for both passenger and goods traffic. An eighth station was soon provided at Redhurst for the benefit of local dairy farmers who were loath to cart their ponderous 17 gallon milk churns to the neighbouring stations at Thor's Cave or Wetton Mill. However, the precise status of this eighth station was never entirely clear, and for the first few years Redhurst was regarded as nothing more than a milk platform. It did not appear in North Staffordshire timetables until the middle of World War I, but the July 1916 Working Timetable shows that passenger trains were, by that time, stopping there on an 'as required' basis.

Lengths of standard gauge trackwork were installed at some Leek & Manifold stations in order that full-size freight stock could be accommodated, but none of the intermediate stations had goods sheds, cattle docks or weigh-houses. Those stations equipped with 4 ft 8½ in. gauge sidings could, generally speaking, hold just two or three short wheelbase standard gauge wagons, the length of full size trackwork at each location being about 68 ft long in each case. Hulme End, in contrast, could accommodate about a dozen main line wagons in two, somewhat longer, sidings.

The newly-opened narrow gauge line was laid with flat-bottomed rail secured to transverse wooden sleepers, and many of the sharpest curves were check-railed. The steepest gradients were 1 in 41 on the approaches to Waterhouses and 1 in 50 between Wetton Mill and Butterton; the principal engineering feature was the 164 yds-long tunnel at Swainsley, and there were numerous underline bridges at places where the winding single line crossed the rivers Hamps or Manifold. These were, in most cases, formed of lightweight girders resting on stone abutments, central piers being added where necessary. The tunnel was bored through solid rock, the original intention being that it would be unlined; when, at a later stage of construction, it was decided that a double ring of brickwork would be inserted the effective width of the tunnel was reduced from 14 ft 3 in. to 12 ft. The line was ballasted with material salvaged from the spoil tips at Ecton, and most commentators agreed with The Railway Magazine's view that the line was 'laid in the most substantial manner'.

At Waterhouses the line ended in an interchange station with separate platforms for the 2 ft 6 in. and 4 ft 8½ in. gauge traffic. Unfortunately, the unfinished state of the North Staffordshire branch from Leek meant that passengers had to use a temporary station on the outskirts of the village. A simple wooden shack had been erected for use as a station building, but there were no run-round facilities and trains had to draw forward into the goods yard in order to run-round at the end of each journey from Hulme End. (This first temporary station was used until the opening of the NSR branch on 1st July, 1905, on which day L&MVLR trains started carrying passengers to and from the joint North Staffordshire-Leek & Manifold station.)

Like many other narrow gauge railways the Leek & Manifold line was built as cheaply and economically as possible, and to save expense all road crossings were on the level. The level crossing at Waterhouses was fully gated and protected by rudimentary signals, but elsewhere, most roads or tracks crossed the line at unprotected crossings – this method of operation being allowed because as a light railway the Leek & Manifold line was subject to very strict speed restrictions. The five ungated public level crossings mentioned in Major Druitt's report were equipped with cattle grids, but ordinary occupation crossings were 'gated' in the sense that farmers were expected to open and close the gates before crossing the line

(these gates did not close across the line as they did at the proper level crossing at Waterhouses).

The line was, from its inception, worked by the North Staffordshire Railway under the operating agreement made prior to opening; the railway and all its equipment remained the property of the L&MVLR, but tickets, timetables, waybills and other items necessary for the operation of the railway were supplied by the operating company. The station master at Hulme End and other railway staff were employees of the NSR, and photographic evidence suggests that these men wore standard North Staffordshire uniforms with that company's badges and insignia. The line nevertheless had its own liveries for locomotives and rolling stock (at least in the early years), and the Leek & Manifold Board of Directors continued to meet.

The First Twelve Months

In organisational terms, the system under which the NSR worked the line should have worked smoothly in that the larger company was responsible for everyday operation while the Leek & Manifold company was left with responsibility for the payment of debts incurred during construction and the apportioning of dividends (if and when any were paid). Unfortunately, the system did not always work effectively because the L&MVLR Directors saw fit to disagree with the NSR on a whole range of issues. There was, moreover, a certain amount of friction between the two companies over mundane issues such as the lack of toilets at the intermediate stations. This problem was raised at a Leek & Manifold Directors' meeting held on 16th November, 1904, and after discussion the Secretary was asked to obtain estimates for the building of 'earth closets at the stations'. The 'earth closets' were apparently in place in time for the following summer traffic, but on 21st June, 1905 the Directors resolved that the toilets should be placed 'in a less prominent position'.[18]

Despite these difficulties the first months of operation were modestly successful, though at the height of the summer season the North Staffordshire complained that there was insufficient rolling stock on the new line. This problem was exacerbated by an accident that took place in August 1904; the precise details of this incident are unclear, but it is known that two of the L&MVLR's four coaches were rendered unfit for service at the time when they were most needed. The accident was mentioned at a Directors' meeting held on 31st August, 1904, the relevant entry in the Leek & Manifold minute book being as follows:

> Reference was made to the accident to the new coaches. The Secretary explained that No. 3 coach had been repaired by the contractors at Hulme End and that No. 4 coach had to be returned to the makers for repairs. The question of liability for the damage was left to the makers.[15]

The minutes do not, unfortunately, elaborate on this incident, but the reference to liability suggests that the vehicles may not have been legally handed-over to the L&MVLR at the time that the damage was sustained. One possibility is that the coaches were damaged in transit to the Leek &

Manifold line – there may, for instance, have been a collision or breakaway when the two new coaches were placed on the line (in which case the L&MVLR would not have been liable).

Another problem that appeared during the first few months concerned the 'one-engine-in-steam' system of operation. It appears that the arrangements referred to by Major Druitt whereby the ground frame at Hulme End was worked by a key attached to the train staff were unsatisfactory. There was, in particular, an overwhelming problem in that, once the train staff had been sent out with an up train there was no means of unlocking the frame at Hulme End! This meant that the station could not effectively be operated when the train was in the section, and in an attempt to solve this problem the North Staffordshire operating authorities asked the Board of Trade for permission to work the line on the train-staff-and-ticket system.[20] The BoT agreed to this mode of operation in 1906, and thereafter the line could be worked with two trains on the line at any one time.

Waterhouses temporary station prior to opening day.   *Locomotive Publishing Co.*

Chapter Three
The Line in Operation (1905–1934)

The original train service of three trains each way (with extra workings on Saturdays and market days) was maintained throughout the first months of operation, but in December 1904 a much reduced winter train service was introduced. The North Staffordshire Railway felt that the line could best be worked on Saturdays and market days only, and in consequence the Manifold Valley route was operated on just two days a week. This mode of operation was a cost efficient way of working the line during the winter months, but the Leek & Manifold Directors argued that their railway should be worked every weekday throughout the year, and a winter service of two up and two down trains was soon reintroduced.

The Leek–Waterhouses Bus Service

Although the Great Western Railway is generally regarded as an important pioneer in the field of road feeder services, it should not be forgotten that many other railways were also prepared to conduct experiments in the field of steam or petrol-driven road vehicles, and in this context it is interesting to say a little more about the North Staffordshire Railway's road feeder service between Leek and Waterhouses.

The service was introduced on 29th June, 1904, when two 35 hp steam buses commenced running three up and three down trips in connection with the Leek & Manifold trains at Waterhouses. The journey time was 60 minutes in each direction and the single fare was 8d. The two buses could accommodate just 22 passengers, and in view of this limited capacity priority was given to people wishing to travel through to Hulme End or other destinations by train. The buses were built by Straker & Co. of Bristol, and they were painted in NSR livery with the company's famous loose knot badge on each side. These unusual vehicles had iron-tyred wheels, and access to the passenger saloon was by means of a platform at the rear end.

The Leek to Waterhouses road service came to an end with the belated completion of the North Staffordshire branch between Leek, Ipstones and Waterhouses on 1st July, 1905, and thereafter the Leek & Manifold timetable was altered slightly in an attempt to provide convenient connecting services for people travelling between Leek, Waterhouses and Hulme End by train.

Operating the Line in the Edwardian Period

The new timetable was similar to that in operation prior to July 1905, and the basic weekday train service still provided three up and three down workings between Hulme End and Waterhouses. The first up train left Hulme End at 8.40 am and reached Waterhouses at 9.20, allowing through travellers to change into a North Staffordshire Railway branch train for the remainder of their journey to Leek (arr. 10.00 am). The locomotive and train set that had worked the 8.40 am returned to the upper terminus at 9.35 am, and there was then an enormous gap in the timetable until the next up train left Hulme End at 2.10 pm; this train arrived in Waterhouses at 2.50, in good

North Staffordshire Railway.

LEEK & WATERHOUSES

OMNIBUS SERVICE

COMMENCING JUNE 29th, and until AUGUST 31st.

The Motor Omnibus, in connection with the Trains on the Manifold Valley Light Railway, will run between Leek and Waterhouses in connection with Trains to and from the North Staffordshire System, as shewn below

TIME TABLE.

		a.m.	a.m.	Thursdays and Saturdays only p.m.	Thursdays and Saturdays p.m.	Thursdays and Saturdays p.m.			a.m.	p.m.	p.m.	Thursdays and Saturdays only p.m.
Leek · · · dep.		8 50	11 15	2 15	5 0	7 25	Waterhouses · dep.		10 5	12 35	6 15	8 40
Bradnop · about		9 8	11 33	2 33	5 18	7 43	Winkhill · about		10 20	12 50	6 30	8 55
Bottom House ..		9 26	11 51	2 51	5 36	8 1	Bottom House ..		10 24	12 54	6 34	9 0
Winkhill · - ..		9 30	11 55	2 55	5 40	8 5	Bradnop - · ..		10 42	1 12	6 52	9 18
Waterhouses · arr		9 50	12 15	3 15	6 0	8 25	Leek · - arr.		11 5	1 35	7 15	9 40

Passengers will be allowed to take luggage not exceeding 28 lbs. without charge at their own risk. Packages exceeding 28 lbs. will not be conveyed.

The Motor Omnibus will accommodate 22 Passengers only. and not more than that number can be accepted for conveyance ; and in all cases preference will be given to Passengers arriving and going forward by Train.

Stoke-on-Trent, June, 1904.   W. D. PHILLIPPS, General Manager.

Timetable for the omnibus service used to connect passengers between the Leek and Waterhouses stations.   *British Railways*

time for through travellers to catch the 3.10 pm NSR service to Leek. After waiting at Waterhouses for just ten minutes the Manifold Valley train returned to Hulme End at 3.00 pm, and after a 45 minute journey this second down working arrived at its destination. Finally, at 4.25 pm the train made its third and last trip to Waterhouses, and having arrived at 5.05 pm, the train set off for Hulme End at 5.15 pm.

On Thursdays and Saturdays this basic pattern of operation was amended to permit an enhanced service of four up and four down trains, with departures from Hulme End at 8.40, 10.35 am, 1.25 and 7.45 pm and balancing down workings from Waterhouses at 9.35, 11.30 am, 2.25 and 8.40 pm respectively. The service was maintained with just one locomotive and train set, though at times of particularly heavy traffic both engines might be used on trains of up to ten loaded vehicles (i.e. the four coaches plus up to six goods vehicles). Loops were available at Wetton Mill and Ecton for Warslow, but these facilities would not have been used for passing purposes because the line's signalling system did not permit two trains to cross intermediately on the single line (see Chapter Five).

The Manifold line soon became popular as a venue for excursionists from the smoke-laden towns of the Potteries, but the North Staffordshire operating authorities were reluctant to provide a Sunday service, and although some Sunday workings were initially provided, the NSR withdrew the Sunday trains altogether in the winter of 1906. This led to friction between the North Stafford and Manifold Valley companies, and a limited Sunday service was eventually reinstated; one reason for running such trains was the necessity of providing a 7-day a week service for local dairy farmers (who would otherwise have despatched their milk to London via the rival London & North Western route from Hartington).

There was much friction between the North Staffordshire Railway and the L&MVLR over the contentious matter of winter operation, but in the event the Leek & Manifold Directors were able to persuade the NSR that the line should be kept fully operational throughout the year. There were, on the other hand, considerable differences between the summer and winter time-tables – the line being much busier during the peak holiday months of July and August than at other times of the year.

The summer 1908 timetable was one of the fullest ever provided on the Leek & Manifold line, the busiest day of the week being Saturday when the basic service of three return trips between Hulme End and Waterhouses was increased to six up and seven down workings. Wednesdays and Thursdays were also quite busy days, with five or six trains in each direction, while on Mondays the summer timetable offered local travellers a choice of four up and four down services. On Tuesdays, Fridays and Sundays the 1908 timetable provided three trains in each direction, the Sunday workings being arranged so that excursionists from Leek or the Potteries could catch the first down train from Waterhouses at 12.25 pm and then spend an afternoon at Thor's Cave, Beeston Tor or some of the other beauty spots served by the Leek & Manifold Valley line.

In practice, the 1908 summer timetable must be seen as one of the most complex ever seen on the L&MVLR, and whereas during the slack winter months the line could easily have been operated by just one engine and

Two views of the Steam omnibuses (built by Strakers of Bristol) used on the service connecting Leek and Waterhouses, until the mainline via Bradings station was opened. *L.&.G.R.P. Collection, courtesy of David and Charles*

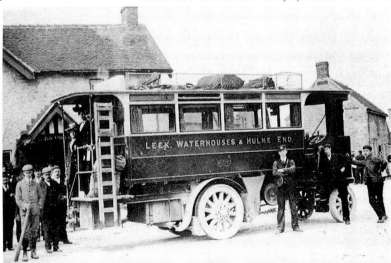

perhaps one passenger vehicle, the 1908 timetable suggests that both engines would have been needed to work the line during the peak holiday months of July and August. The times of arrival and departure from Waterhouses and Hulme End were (in 1908) as shown below:

		MWSO	WThSO	SO	ThO	WSO	ThO			ThSO
		am	am	pm	pm	pm	pm	pm	pm	pm	pm
Hulme End	dep.	8.40	10.35	1.00	–	–	–	–	4.25	6.15	8.00
Waterhouses	arr.	9.20	11.15	1.40	–	–	–	–	5.05	6.55	8.40
Waterhouses	dep.	9.35	11.30	–	2.00	2.10	2.50	3.00	5.20	7.05	9.00
Hulme End	arr.	10.15	12.10	–	2.40	2.50	3.30	3.40	6.00	7.45	9.40

Careful study of the above timings will reveal that the 8.40, 10.35 (MWSO), 4.25, 6.15 and 8.00 pm (ThSO) workings were simple out-and-back trips between Hulme End and Waterhouses, but the 1.00 pm (WThSO) service was not balanced by any corresponding down train. On Saturdays the locomotive and rolling stock were worked back to Hulme End as the 2.00 pm (SO) down service, while on Wednesdays the early afternoon down train left at 2.50 pm. There was, however, a similar 2.50 pm down service on Saturdays, while on Thursdays there were return workings to Hulme End at 2.10 pm and 3.00pm – in other words, on Thursdays and Saturdays the 1.00 pm up train was balanced by two return workings.

As there was no other means of getting an engine from Hulme End to Waterhouses it appears that the 1.00 pm up working must have been a double-headed formation which later divided at Waterhouses to form the two down services. Alternatively, there may have been an unadvertised empty or light engine working between Hulme End and Waterhouses; photographic evidence does, in fact, show that double-heading was frequently resorted to on the L&MVLR, and it seems more likely that this operational problem would have been solved by the simple expedient of coupling both engines together and running them to Waterhouses as one train.

Winter timetables were less intensive than those in operation during the busy summer months, but there were still many variations between 'market' days and other days. In October 1906, for instance, there were two trains each way on normal days, but on Wednesdays trains left Hulme End for Waterhouses at 8.40, 10.35 am, 1.40 and 4.35 pm, with return workings from Waterhouses at 9.35, 11.25 am, 2.40 and 5.35 pm respectively.

The Saturday service was similar, the one difference between Wednesdays and Saturdays being the addition of an extra return trip from Hulme End to Waterhouses at 7.00 pm (returning at 7.50 pm). Confusingly, the Thursday timetable was somewhat different to that in operation on other days of the week, with departures from Hulme End at 8.40 am, 2.00, 4.15 and 6.15 pm and corresponding down workings from Waterhouses at 9.35 am, 2.50, 5.35 and 7.05pm.

The winter timetable persisted, with only minor variations, throughout the Edwardian period, and in October 1914 there were still two trains in each direction with two additional return workings on Wednesdays. On Saturdays, there was just one additional train from Hulme End to Water-

No. 1 *E.R. Calthrop* poses for the camera at Hulme End. The gentleman in the battered bush hat is thought to be John Earle, the resident engineer.   *Lens of Sutton*

A 3-coach train pauses at Thor's Cave shortly after opening; the original refreshment room can be seen (*left*) and Thor's Cave itself is in the background. The refreshment room was later taken to Wetton village and used as a reading room!   *Lens of Sutton*

houses at 1.25 pm (returning at 2.30 pm) but the Saturday evening working no longer ran; on Sundays, the local farmers were served by just one train in each direction which left Hulme End at 5.00 pm and arrived back at the upper terminus by 6.55 pm.

Sadly, the Leek & Manifold company was never a financial success, and although summer excursion traffic developed satisfactorily during the early years the line failed to build-up an appreciable goods or mineral business. Hopes that a rail link would stimulate a revival of the local copper mining industry were wildly optimistic, and in contrast to many other narrow gauge railways (for example the Festiniog or Vale of Rheidol lines) the Leek & Manifold Valley Light Railway eked out a meagre existence as a mainly passenger-orientated route. One hopeful sign, as far as freight traffic was concerned, was the gradual development of milk and other types of agri-cultural traffic, while sales of surplus stone from the spoil tips at Ecton contributed further income for the struggling company.

Extension to Buxton?

One solution to the Leek & Manifold's problems might have been a policy of extension towards Buxton, and indeed the company did, at one time, hope to continue its existing line northwards via Longnor, Hollingsborough and Harper Hill. Sadly, the North Staffordshire Railway was unwilling to support the proposed extension scheme, and neighbouring landowners were, in any case, opposed to the idea of a Buxton to Hulme End line. An attempt to involve the London & North Western Railway in this venture having proved abortive, the Leek & Manifold Directors were forced to abandon the Buxton scheme – though the project was still being discussed around 1911.

The Buxton extension was never made, but it is interesting to recall that in 1909 a subsidised bus service was established between Stoke, Hulme End and Buxton; the service ran about three times a day during the summer season, the return charabanc fare between Buxton and Hulme End being three shillings. This road motor service was modestly successful, but the buses ran for just one season; in theory the Leek & Manifold Railway should have received 25 per cent of the net takings, but the NSR claimed this 25 per cent for themselves and although the private bus operator (who owned the vehicles) was willing to provide a similar service in 1910, the North Staffordshire Railway effectively vetoed the scheme.[21]

The North Staffordshire's attitude over this matter was a reflection of the strained relationships pertaining between the NSR and Leek & Manifold companies at this time – the underlying problem being, as always, the Manifold company's chronic financial difficulties. The L&MVLR proprietors had been obliged (on more than one occasion) to renegotiate their operating agreement with the North Staffordshire Railway, and attempts to induce the NSR to purchase the line having failed, the Leek & Manifold Directors were forced to issue further 4 per cent debenture stock in order to pay off some of their existing loans!

It was felt (perhaps unjustly) that the North Staffordshire was making a healthy profit out of the Leek & Manifold line, but in reality, the railway was

LEEK, WATERHOUSES, and HULME END (Manifold Valley Light).—North Staffordshire.

Passenger Timetable for Oct 1906

Passenger Timetable for Oct 1908

Passenger Timetable for July 1922

Passenger Timetable for 1931

LEEK, WATERHOUSES, and HULME END (Manifold Valley Light).—North Staffordshire.

Week Days. *Suns.*

Stations: Leek, Bradnop, Ipstones, Waterhouses, Hulme End

Notes: "Halts" at Caldon Low, between Waterhouses, and at Sparrow Cave, Beeston Cave, Wetton, Grindon, Thor's Cave, Wetton Mill, Butterton, and Ecton. Mill, Butterton, and Ecton Tickets. Warslow, between Waterhouses and Hulme End. Waterhouses Tickets are available at Caldon Low.
e Except Saturdays. s Saturdays only. † Station for Hartington.

LEEK, WATERHOUSES, and HULME END—Manifold Valley Light (1st and 3rd class).—North Staffordshire.

Stations: Leek, Bradnop, Ipstones, Waterhouses, Hulme End

Mons., Weds. and Sats. / SUNDAYS. / Weds. & Sats. only. / Sats. only. / Thurs. only.

z Mondays only. x Except Mondays. y Thursdays and Saturdays, z Weds., Thurs., and Sats. † Station for Sheen and Hartington.
"Halts" at Caldon Low, between Ipstones and Waterhouses, and at Sparrowlee, Beeston Tor, Grindon, Thor's Cave, Wetton Mill, Butterton, and Ecton.
(for Warslow), between Waterhouses and Hulme End. Waterhouse Tickets are available at Caldon Low.

LEEK, WATERHOUSES, and HULME END.—North Staffordshire.

Third class only between Leek and Waterhouses.

Week Days. / Suns. / Wednesdays and Saturdays. / Saturdays only.

Stations: Leek, Bradnop, Ipstones, Sparrowlee, Beeston Tor, Grindon, Thor's Cave, Redhurst Crossing, Wetton Mill, Butterton, Ecton, for Warslow, Hulme End

Waterhouses Tickets are available at Caldon Low Halt.
‡‡ Stops when required. * Station for Wetton. † Station for Sheen (1¼ miles) and Hartington (1¾ miles).

LEEK, WATERHOUSES, and HULME END.

One class only between Leek and Waterhouses.

Week Days only.

Stations: Leek, Bradnop, Ipstones, Waterhouses, Sparrowlee, Beeston Tor, Grindon, Thor's Cave, Redhurst Crossing, Wetton Mill, Butterton, Ecton, for Warslow, Hulme End

A Station for Wetton. Aa Stops when required. B Station for Sheen (1¼ miles) and Hartington (1¾ miles).
"Halts" at Winkhill and at Caldon Low between Ipstones and Waterhouses.

HULME END, WATERHOUSES, and LEEK.

One class only between Waterhouses and Leek.

Week Days only. / Wednesdays only.

Stations: Hulme End, Ecton, for Warslow, Butterton, Wetton Mill, Redhurst Crossing, Thor's Cave, Grindon, Beeston Tor, Sparrowlee, Waterhouses, Ipstones, Bradnop, Leek

A Station for Wetton. Aa Stops when required. P Passengers holding Waterhouses tickets will be allowed to join or alight at Caldon Low Halt; those wishing to alight must give notice to Guard.
"Halts" at Caldon Low and at Winkhill, between Waterhouses and Ipstones.

not a paying concern; its traffic was never sufficient to pay off the large debts incurred during the construction of the line, and in these melancholy circumstances the undertaking can never have paid its way.

World War I

Matters had reached an *impasse* by 1914, but in that year the outbreak of World War I pushed relatively minor problems such as the Leek & Manifold Railway's finances into the background, and like all other British railways, the line settled down to play an important part in the national war effort.

Railways were taken into government control at the start of the conflict, and for the next few years the L&MVLR was operated with a reduced timetable to serve the needs of the local community. In July 1916, for example, the inhabitants of the Manifold Valley were served by just two trains each way, though on Wednesdays there were two additional workings to convey market day traffic. A similar situation pertained on Saturdays, when the ordinary 8.40 am and 4.25 pm services from Hulme End were augmented by two extra return workings at 1.25 and 6.5 pm. On Sundays there was one train in each direction – primarily to cater for the dairy farmers who relied on the railway to provide a seven-day service.

Milk production was, in fact, of great importance during the 1914–18 conflict, and at a time when British farmers were being urged to help the war effort, the Leek & Manifold line carried increasing numbers of 17-gallon milk churns throughout the war. Some idea of the volume of milk conveyed at this time will be apparent when one considers that in 1911 approximately 220,000 gallons of mile had been conveyed over the L&MVLR, whereas by 1918 this annual figure had risen to no less than 590,000 gallons.[21]

Half a million gallons of milk was a modest enough figure when compared to the amounts of milk carried regularly on some Great Western branch lines during the early 1900s, but it presented a problem for the North Stafford-shire operating authorities in that the L&MVLR had very few vehicles in which the heavy churns could be carried (the two open wagons and the box van being the most suitable). There were, therefore, suggestions that NSR milk vans could be carried on the transporter cars, and after suitable modifi-cations had been made the railway commenced carrying 4 or 6-wheeled standard gauge vans through to L&MVLR stations. Later, modern glass-lined milk tankers were conveyed to a new dairy and cheese factory that was opened at Ecton after the war.

In 1915 the Leek & Manifold Railway suffered a major blow with the death of Colonel Charles Bill, the company Chairman. Colonel Bill had, for several years, supported the unremunerative railway with his own money, and in these circumstances the loss of such a generous supporter was a matter of grave concern; the Colonel was replaced, as Chairman, by A.J. Hambleton.

The Great War came to an end on 11th November, 1918, but damaging coal and railway strikes meant that the immediate post-war years were far from happy ones. Moreover, the insidious growth of road transport posed a new and growing threat to lightly-used rural lines such as the Manifold Valley route, and made their future increasingly insecure.

There was, nevertheless, a gradual return to pre-war conditions, and by 1921 summer tourist traffic was once again providing a useful source of revenue for the Leek & Manifold line. The North Staffordshire Railway collaborated with the L&MVLR by running summer excursion trains to Waterhouses and advertising the many attractions of the Manifold Valley area, and for a few more years at least, the Leek & Manifold Railway continued to function as a local tourist attraction.

The post-war summer timetables were less complex than those in operation prior to 1914, but an increased train service was still provided. In July 1922, for example, there were return trips from Hulme End to Waterhouses at 8.55 am, 4.05 pm and 7.05 pm, with one extra service on Wednesdays and two on Saturdays. All trains connected with NSR branch trains at Waterhouses, typical journey times, for the 18 mile through journey to Leek being around 1½ hours inclusive of the intermediate change.

This timetable presented few operational problems, and, even on Saturdays, the service could be maintained by just one locomotive and train set, working a series of out and back trips from Hulme End. The basic method of operation was as follows:

		SO	WSO				Sun
		am	am	pm	pm	pm	pm
Hulme End	dep.	8.55	10.50	1.25	4.05	7.05	3.40
Waterhouses	arr.	9.35	11.30	2.05	4.50	7.50	4.20
Waterhouses	dep.	9.50	11.56	2.35	5.30	8.20	5.05
Hulme End	arr.	10.30	12.30	3.15	6.10	9.00	5.45

It will be seen that this pattern of services offered no more than five trains each way, even on Saturdays (compared with six up and seven down in 1908). The most important difference between the summer timetables of 1908 and 1922 was, however, the balanced nature of the 1922 service – trains simply ran from Hulme End to Waterhouses and then back again. A further point which might be made is that there were no freight workings, as such, on the Leek & Manifold line. What little freight traffic presented itself was conveyed in 'mixed' formations consisting of one or two passenger vehicles and perhaps two loaded transporter wagons. If any shunting was necessary at an intermediate station the passengers were left waiting while their engine busied itself positioning the freight vehicle for unloading (at Ecton the engine ambled off down the branch to the creamery – much to the surprise of uninitiated travellers!).

It is generally accepted that World War I marked the end of an era – not only for the old time railway companies but also for British society as a whole. This was certainly the case with the Leek & Manifold Railway, which was never quite the same after 1914–18. Quite apart from the adverse effects of road competition, the company itself had changed perceptibly, many of the grand old men who had nurtured the railway in its formative years having passed away. As we have seen, the L&MVLR suffered a grievous loss with the death of Charles Bill (at the age of 70) on 9th December, 1915, but this was not the only blow because Sir Thomas Wardle had died (aged 78) on 3rd January, 1909, while John Sheldon – another staunch supporter of the railway – died on 23rd August, 1913.

The loss of these long-standing supporters within a comparatively short space of time can have done little to cheer the surviving Directors – who were now having to admit that the Leek & Manifold Railway was probably the most unsuccessful of all the railways promoted under the provisions of the 1896 Light Railway Act. In recognition of this unhappy fact the operating agreement with the North Staffordshire Company had been amended so that, by the 1920s, the NSR was paying the L&MVLR just £725 per annum for the dubious distinction of operating the loss-making line. The agreement was due to end in 1926, but external events were destined to intervene before that particular problem could be faced.

The Grouping and After

In Victorian times successive governments had opposed large scale railway amalgamation on the grounds that competition between smaller companies would result in greater efficiency. The trauma of World War I had, however, left all railways in a run-down condition, and in the changed conditions pertaining after 1918 the government decided that the interests of the nation would best be served if the main line companies were 'grouped' into four large regional companies. Accordingly, on 1st January, 1923 the 'Big Four' railways were created under the provisions of the Transport Act 1921, and as a result of this great amalgamation the number of British railway companies was reduced from 58 to just 20 (*i.e.* the Big Four companies plus 16 smaller undertakings). As far as the Leek & Manifold Valley Light Railway was concerned, the 1923 grouping heralded the end of an era because both the North Staffordshire and L&MVLR companies became an integral part of the London Midland & Scottish Railway.

A Diesel Electric railcar constructed for the Gaekwar's Baroda State Railway, India seen here undergoing trials on the Leek & Manifold Railway.

Courtesy Railway Magazine

In retrospect, the grouping heralded the demise of the Leek & Manifold Railway; the LMS was a large conglomerate with little interest in curiosities such as the Manifold line, and although the new company was prepared to exploit holiday traffic on other parts of its vast system, the LMS authorities seemed reluctant to publicise the picturesque (but comparatively little-known) Manifold Valley area.

In the short term the 1923 grouping produced few obvious changes, and most ordinary travellers would have been unaware that a change of owner-ship had in fact taken place. In the ensuing months, however, the LMS introduced new liveries for locomotives and rolling stock, the engines appearing in lined red (later replaced by unadorned black) while passenger vehicles were painted in a crimson lake livery with the letters 'LMS' in small lettering. Freight rolling stock, meanwhile, was presumably repainted in LMS mid-grey livery. All of the Leek & Manifold rolling stock was re-numbered under LMS auspices, the numbers chosen being 14989–14992 for passenger vehicles and 195311–195318 for freight rolling stock. The full numbering scheme was as follows:

LMS Nos.	Vehicle Type	
14989	42 ft	brake composite
14990	42 ft	brake composite
14991	42 ft	third class coach
14992	42 ft	third class coach
195311	19.5 ft	transporter wagon
195312	19.5 ft	transporter wagon
195313	19.5 ft	transporter wagon
195314	31 ft	'long' transporter wagon
195315	'short'	transporter wagon
195316	25 ft	bogie goods van
195317	25 ft	bogie open wagon
195318	25 ft	bogie open wagon

At the time of its creation in 1923 the LMS owned a significant narrow gauge mileage, and in addition to the 8¾ mile Leek & Manifold line the company inherited over 47 miles of 3 ft gauge lines in County Antrim (as well as being a co-owner of the extensive County Donegal 3 ft gauge system). This narrow gauge mileage was further extended in 1924–5 when the LMS Northern Counties Committee purchased the 16 miles-long Ballycastle Railway. Sadly, the LMS showed little interest in its narrow gauge assets, and there was very little investment in these picturesque, but remote routes. The County Antrim lines, for instance, were allowed to run-down, and there were large scale closures in the early 1930s (though most of the 3 ft gauge lines remained open for occasional freight traffic).

Towards Closure

The fate of the Leek & Manifold line reflected that of the once-extensive County Antrim branches, in that, in both cases, the LMS showed little inclination to renew trackwork or other vital equipment. Neither did the company make any real attempt to publicise the Manifold Valley route, and railway enthusiasts feared that the line was being run-down prior to complete closure.

As we have seen, the Leek & Manifold line had never been financially successful, and by the early 1920s the annual loss was said to be £2,000. In summertime the line was still moderately busy with tourist traffic, but there were few other sources of revenue, and the short summer season could not sustain the railway throughout the rest of the year. The 1930s were, more-over, a period of acute financial stringency, and at a time when the 'Big Four' companies were closing unremunerative branch lines in increasing numbers the future for the Manifold route looked increasingly precarious.

The one reliable source of traffic at this time was milk, which was conveyed from the creamery at Ecton in standard gauge milk tanks mounted on the L&MR transporter wagons. There was also a small traffic in milk churns, these being carried in the bogie goods van or on the open wagons. Sadly, this lucrative source of traffic came to an end with the closure of Ecton Creamery in 1932 and the simultaneous opening of a new centralised dairy at neighbouring Rowsley; local farmers began to send their milk to this new facility by road, and with the cessation of this last regular flow of freight traffic, the Leek & Manifold Railway lost its reason for existence.

The train service provided during the final years of the line consisted of two trains each way throughout the year, rising to three up and three down workings during the summer tourist season; the Sunday service comprised one train in each direction. The amount of holiday traffic carried during the early 1930s was very small, and H.C. Casserley – who knew the line at this time – considered that tourist traffic had 'gradually dwindled almost to vanishing point'. Occasionally, some enterprising motor coach operator would arrange a combined rail–road excursion, the usual pattern being for trippers to be conveyed to Waterhouses or Hulme End by road for a single journey on the line; the motor coach would, in the meantime, run empty to the other end of the line in order to meet the excursionists at the end of their scenic ride along the picturesque Manifold Valley.

The 2 ft 6 in. gauge trackwork had not been renewed for over 20 years, but the riding qualities of Everard Calthrop's magnificent narrow gauge bogie coaches never deteriorated, and Mr Casserley remembered that the L&MVLR vehicles were 'exceedingly comfortable and smooth riding';[22] the Manifold trains were, he thought, among the best that he had ever travelled on – even at the very end.

Another glimpse of the Leek & Manifold Railway during its declining years comes from the pen of Mr W.T.F. Castle, who, in 1930, won a 'holiday letters' competition sponsored by the *Model Railway News*. He recalled that, having heard of the beauties of the Manifold valley, he had taken a holiday in the area to see the line for himself. After a trip from Leek to Waterhouses behind former North Staffordshire 'D' class 0–6–0T No. 1597, he joined the L&MVLR at Waterhouses; the Manifold train consisted of one of the two 2–6–4Ts 'and two centre-gangway saloons, with an LNER 12-ton wagon containing 10 tons of Worthington for the little pub at Hulme End'. Hulme End was, he thought, 'a nice little station with one platform, two-road loco depot, water tank and crane, two-road carriage shed, loading gauges and two-arm signal'.[23] On the return journey, the train called at Ecton to pick up two United Dairies milk tankers.

As mentioned above, the closure of Ecton dairy deprived the railway of its one remaining source of traffic and this – together with the need to spend thousands of pounds on track renewals – led directly to the closure of the line. There was little protest at this decision; railway enthusiasts hoped that the route might be retained as a summer-only holiday line, but the LMS was not as committed to leisure traffic as the Great Western, and whereas the GWR might have introduced some system whereby holiday traffic could have been carried (as it did on the Vale of Rheidol Line) the LMS operating authorities decided to close the line in its entirety. It was announced that the railway would cease operation on and from Monday 12th March, 1934, and as there was no Sunday service, the last trains ran on Saturday 10th March, 1934.

Closure of the Line

The last day of the Leek & Manifold Valley Light Railway was cold and dismal, the misery of the occasion being heightened by mist, and snowy weather conditions. The closure was a subdued affair, and few enthusiasts turned up to ride on the final trains. Mr D.M. Smith was, however, determined to see the line on its last day, and after a long and complicated overnight journey from Euston to Manchester and thence to Leek, he arrived in time to catch the first down train from Waterhouses to Hulme End:

> Both Leek and Waterhouses were beneath a three-inch blanket of snow, and this promised for those who were to make the journey the good fortune of seeing the Manifold Valley, one of the most lovely in England, in the most beautiful conditions.
>
> After much shunting, the little train, composed of one passenger car and two or three goods vehicles, left Waterhouses almost half-an-hour late with only seven passengers. We were not even promised that the train would never be late again! Soon we had puffed and rattled through the valley of the Hamps and entered that of the Manifold. Here, in the stillness and silence the snow lay thick, while the tops of the 400 ft valley sides were clothed in a soft white mist. Only one stop was made during the eight-mile journey, a passenger alighting at Grindon Halt. The atmosphere of the valley was amazing, and the gaunt pinnacle of Thor's Cave, sinister in its predominance on any other day, rose mysteriously fairylike into the softening mist.
>
> At Hulme End, the terminus, reality returned, for it seemed as if we had passed through a valley of dreams. There was considerable activity here – a place which consists of several cottages and a Light Railway Hotel, now, alas, an anachronism – as after all, even on a light railway the last day of service must have a certain importance. Station equipment had to be collected and returned; incidentally, many of the tickets that were being issued were of the pre-grouping era North Staffordshire Railway era. The rolling stock and buildings, on the other hand, were, so far as the staff was concerned, to be abandoned as they stood, and instructions had been received that the two locomotives, one of which returned from an overhauling at Crewe only three weeks before, should be greased and left in the sheds. The staff was being transferred to other parts of the LMS system, and a wry smile from a cleaner was the only answer to the suggestion that this might mean rather more work than that entailed in the running of two trains a day.[24]

Locomotive *E.R. Calthrop* heads a demolition train on the doomed line near Thor's Cave.   *Lens of Sutton*

Another view of *E.R. Calthrop* at work on the demolition contract.   *H.N. James*

After the last public service had been run, the Leek & Manifold rolling stock was shunted into Waterhouses goods yard, where it remained for several months; locomotive No. 2 *J.B. Earle* was taken to Crewe Works for possible resale, but No. 1 *E.R. Calthrop* was left at Waterhouses beneath a tarpaulin cover.

Lifting

Lifting of the redundant line was under way by 1937, and in April *The Railway Magazine* reported that the LMS had 'recently sold the two 2 ft 6 in. gauge 2−6−4 tank locomotives Nos. 1 and 2, named *E.R. Calthrop* and *J.B. Earle* respectively, of the former Manifold Valley Light Railway, to the contractor who is removing the permanent way'. The contractors concerned were George Cohen Sons & Co. but any hope that they intended to use the engines on a long term basis were dispelled when *J.B. Earle* was taken to their yard at Stanningley for scrapping.[25]

In the meantime, No. 1 was brought back into service to assist in the demolition of the line, and for several months the 2−6−4T could be seen hauling trains of lifted material on the doomed railway. The demolition train usually consisted of two or three of the transporter wagons and one of the opens – the very low transporters being ideal for the conveyance of lifted rails.

The coaches were broken-up in 1936, and the remaining rolling stock was scrapped as soon as the line was lifted. The same fate befell *E.R. Calthorp*, which was cut-up at Waterhouses at the end of the dismantling contract; one wagon survived – the 'short' transporter was purchased by the Ashover Light Railway in 1935, but sadly, it was too big and heavy for the lightly-built Ashover line, and the vehicle saw little (if any) further use.

The trackbed and bridges of the abandoned Leek & Manifold line were presented to Staffordshire County Council by the LMS, and in the next few months the council spent £6,000 in converting the route into a footpath and bridleway. Station buildings, nameboards, and other relics of the defunct light railway were left *in situ* for the convenience of walkers, and the trackbed itself was asphalted to create a level pathway. Finally, on Friday 23rd July, 1937 the new footpath was formally opened by Sir Josiah Stamp,[26] and the LMS Chairman then handed a deed of gift to the Chairman of Staffordshire County Council – thereby severing for ever the last tenuous links between the Manifold valley and its railway.

The standard gauge link between Leek and Waterhouses outlasted the Manifold line by just one year. This line had traditionally carried excursionists to and from the Leek & Manifold line, and although summer tourist traffic had been in steep decline for many years the closure of the L&MVLR obviously resulted in less traffic over the standard gauge route. The last passenger trains were therefore run at the end of the 1935 summer season, leaving a freight service to and from Waterhouses, which was itself withdrawn in 1943. Thereafter, the branch from Leek was retained to serve Caldon Quarries, and in this form the route has survived until today as the final remnant of the Leek, Caldon Lowe & Hartington Light Railways as authorised in 1899.

Thor's Cave station, six years after closure on 4th April, 1940. Although devoid of track the station is still recognisable. *H.C. Casserley*

A view of Hulme End station in the 1950s after the track had been lifted many years. *Oakwood Collection*

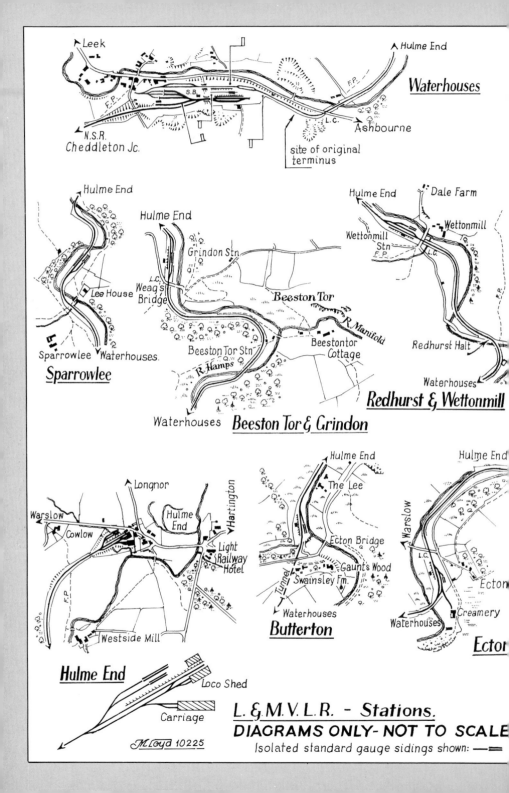

L. & M. V. L. R. – Stations.
DIAGRAMS ONLY – NOT TO SCALE
Isolated standard gauge sidings shown: ━━

Chapter Four
The Stations and Route

It would now be appropriate to describe the stations and route of this interesting narrow gauge line in greater detail, and the following section will take readers on an imaginary guided tour of the Leek & Manifold Railway from Waterhouses to its upper terminus at Hulme End.

Waterhouses

Waterhouses, at the end of the 9¾ mile North Staffordshire branch from Leek, was a station with provision for both standard gauge and 2 ft 6 in. gauge traffic. The standard gauge facilities consisted of a run-round loop, a long dead-end goods siding, and three narrow gauge transhipment sidings in which 4 ft 8½ in. gauge goods vehicles were shunted onto Leek & Manifold transporter wagons.

The narrow gauge platform was situated to the north of the 'main line' station, a short sloping ramp being provided so that travellers could walk between the two halves of the station. The 2 ft 6 in. gauge run-round loop was sited to the west of the station though there was also a short spring loaded passing loop to the east. Three goods sidings were available, and these were entered via the run-round loop; each siding made an end-on junction with its standard gauge counterpart in order that rolling stock could be exchanged between the two systems.

In architectural terms, the wooden station building at Waterhouses resembled those found elsewhere on the North Staffordshire branch line from Leek. A simple, gable-ended structure, it had a low-pitched slated roof, together with a projecting platform canopy that covered only the central part of the building. The platform façade was pierced by two doors and two windows, and there was an external chimney stack at the western end. Careful examination of the weather-boarded walls suggested that the building had been modified at some stage in its life – the likeliest explanation being that the eastern extremity of the station was a later addition.

Having purchased their tickets in the main station building travellers walked down the sloping ramp to the narrow gauge platform, which was equipped with its own waiting room. Lack of space dictated that the latter building was no more than about 6 ft wide, but a generously-proportioned roof was nevertheless provided, and this spanned the full width of the platform – the result being a distinctly 'top-heavy' appearance.

Other buildings at Waterhouses included a wooden goods shed and an ornate signal cabin. The goods shed stood on a raised brick platform, and large double doors enabled general merchandise or other consignments to be loaded or unloaded from an adjacent siding; similar doors in the western gable facilitated transhipment into and out of road vehicles. The nearby signal cabin was conveniently sited between the narrow gauge and the standard gauge lines, in which position it could economically control both halves of the station. A 10-lever frame was sufficient to work the entire layout – the only signals on the 'Manifold' side of the station being the up home and down starting signals at the eastern end of the station complex;

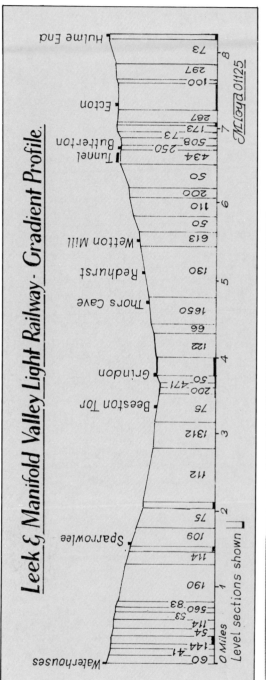

Leek & Manifold Valley Light Railway - Gradient Profile.

Waterhouses — 60 — 41 — 144 — 54 — 114 — 53 — 560 — 83

0 Miles

Level sections shown

— 190 — 1

Sparrowlee — 114 — 109 — 75 — 2

— 112

— 1312 — 3

Beeston Tor — 75

Grindon — 471 — 200 — 50 — 4

— 122 — 66

Thors Cave — 1650

Redhurst — 130 — 5

Wetton Mill — 613

— 50 — 110 — 6 — 200 — 50

Tunnel — 434 — 250 Butterton — 508 — 73 — 7 — 173

Ecton — 287

— 100 — 297 — 8

Hulme End — 73

ℱℒℴℊ∂ 01125

Locomotive No. 1 E.R. Calthrop passes Redhurst Crossing with a mixed train; the milk dock can be glimpsed to the left. *Locomotive Publishing Co.*

Locomotive No. 2 *J.B. Earle* stands in the 'Manifold' platform at Waterhouses, having just arrived with the 3.45 pm from Hulme End on 29th April, 1933.   *H.C. Casserley*

A flag be-decked Waterhouses (temporary station). The banner reads "A Ray of Light Gleams O'er us" on the opening day of the line.   *Locomotive Publishing Company*

Sparrowlee station looking north towards Hulme End on 28th June, 1933; the single goods siding is on the right. Note the unusual nameboard.   H.C. Casserley

A view near Sparrowlee on 28th June, 1933 with bridge No. 10 in the middle distance.
                                                                    H.C. Casserley

Below A characteristic Leek & Manifold bridge near Sparrowlee; the trackwork was laid directly onto the bridge girders.   H.C. Casserley

the line to Leek was worked by electric train staff, but no instruments were needed for the narrow gauge line which, as far as can be ascertained, was always worked as simply as possible by train staff, or staff and ticket.

There were, in addition to the main buildings, a number of smaller stores, sheds and platelayers' huts. Few of these minor structures call for special comment, most being simple gabled sheds of no architectural interest. The goods yard was equipped with a weigh-house, but no yard crane or cattle pens were available; at night, the platforms were illuminated by simple oil lamps positioned in glass lanterns. There was, otherwise, a marked absence of platform furniture – though observant travellers may have noted an unusually large number of 4-wheel luggage trolleys (needed to transfer the heavy 17-gallon milk churns that came to Waterhouses each day).

Waterhouses was little more than a village station, its one and only claim to importance being its function as an interchange point between the Leek & Manifold Railway and the branch from Leek. This former NSR station had no more than half a dozen staff, including porters, signalmen and clerks; there were, on the other hand, at least two permanent way gangs for the narrow and standard gauge lines, and if these extra workers are counted the total number of railway staff based at Waterhouses would have been around 14–16.

Leaving Waterhouses, Leek & Manifold trains faced a brief 1 in 60 descent towards the Ashbourne Road level crossing, and in one place the falling gradient steepened to 1 in 41 – the worst gradient on the entire line. The crossing gates were manually-operated, and as the crossing was about 300 yards from the station it was necessary for a man to be sent out to open the gates whenever a train was expected. The crossing was protected by rotating disc signals which worked in conjunction with the gates (i.e. when the gates were closed the red discs faced incoming trains, but as the gates were opened the discs rotated on a tall shaft so that their red faces could not be seen from the line).

While mentioning the 1 in 41 gradient at Waterhouses, one might add that there were, at one time, fears that this steep incline would result in loco-motive firebox crowns becoming uncovered – and this is another reason why, for so long, both engines ran with their bunkers facing Hulme End. In reality these fears were probably exaggerated, and when E.R. *Calthrop* arrived back from overhaul facing the 'wrong' way there were no obvious problems.

Sparrowlee

Falling steadily on a succession of favourable gradients the single line turned northwards and, with the Hamps River to the right, trains com-menced their scenic journey along the Hamps valley. Crossing the river, the line maintained its northerly heading for the first few miles and, still running downhill on a 1 in 90 gradient, the narrow gauge trains soon rattled past the first mile post between Waterhouses and Hulme End.

A glance to the left revealed the parched, stony bed of the River Hamps, which became a 'real' river only in times of ample rainfall. In fact, the

The curved platform at Beeston Tor looking south towards Waterhouses on 28th June, 1933. The only 'building' here was an old coach body (out of sight to the left of the picture). *H.C. Casserley*

A view along the Leek & Manifold near Beeston Tor on 28th June, 1933.

H.C. Casserley

A sharp curve near Beeston Tor, 3rd May, 1934. *H.C. Casserley*

Hamps flowed underground at this point, the general absence of surface water being an inevitable result of acidic water eating through porous rocks and finding its way into various subterranean holes and cavities. Geologists had long been aware of the presence of 'swallowholes' through which the Hamps and Manifold descended to their underground courses, and Sir Thomas Wardle even attempted to block them up so that tourists could enjoy the sight and sound of a 'proper' river beside the railway! Perhaps fortunately, these experiments were largely unsuccessful, and although Sir Thomas may have marginally increased the amount of surface water the interesting geological phenomenon of the underground rivers was never seriously threatened.

Having followed the east bank of the river for approximately 30 chains, the line deviated to the west bank near Sparrowlee Farm, and after a curve towards the left, trains then crossed back to the eastern side of the dry river – the simple girder bridges provided at these river crossings being of typical Leek & Manifold design. Having reached the east bank once again, trains immediately entered Sparrowlee station, the first intermediate stopping place en route to Hulme End.

Situated just two miles from Waterhouses, Sparrowlee was little more than a halt, with a single platform on the western side of the line and a dead-end goods siding to the east. Like other Leek & Manifold stations Sparrowlee had a very low platform, and its goods siding incorporated a length of 4 ft 8½ in. track upon which standard gauge wagons could be accommodated; the standard gauge line was slightly higher than the 2 ft 6 in. gauge lines – the difference in height being necessary in order that main line vehicles could be rolled onto their narrow gauge transporters.

Facilities for waiting passengers were utterly basic. There was no shelter of any kind, but a seat was positioned on the otherwise open platform and the name SPARROWLEE was displayed on an elaborate nameboard with ornate, scalloped ends. Early timetables show that the station was originally designated 'Sparrowlee for Waterfall', the waterfall referred to being about 1 mile away from the railway. In its Edwardian heyday Sarrowlee became a popular venue for picnic parties, but there were no villages or hamlets in the immediate vicinity and originating traffic was practically nil.

Beeston Tor

Leaving Sparrowlee, northbound trains dropped gradually on a series of falling gradients, the steepest of which was 1 in 75. With wooded hillsides closing-in on both sides the single line meandered through the Hamps Valley and, crossing and recrossing the Hamps River, northbound trains coasted towards Beeston Tor; at this point the line left the Hamps Valley and entered the Manifold Valley – which would provide a relatively easy course for the remainder of the journey to Hulme End.

Beeston Tor station was another tiny halt, with a low platform and an old coach body that served as a shelter and provided scant comfort for the occasional traveller. The only other building at this remote, but picturesque place, was a small refreshment room.

Grindon station looking north after closure. Earl Cathcart's road can be seen to the right.   *H.C. Casserley*

Looking south round the sharp curve seen in the previous photograph, Earl Cathcart's road was built to enable the Earl's tenant farmers to reach the goods siding at Grindon and followed the railway between Beeston Tor and Grindon stations; 3rd May, 1934.
H.C. Casserley

Situated in a particularly remote area, Beeston Tor handled very little traffic. It served the inhabitants of scattered farms and cottages on the neighbouring Throwley estate, but no goods facilities were ever provided here. Instead, the railway company built an access road between Throwley and Grindon stations in order that local farmers could have access to a station with goods facilities; this road was usually referred to as 'Earl Cathcart's Road' because it served the Earl's Throwley estate.

Grindon

From Beeston Tor the route turned north-westwards and commenced a steady climb towards Hulme End, Grindon, the next station, being preceded by a short stretch of 1 in 50 rising gradient and an abrupt 90 degrees curve.

Situated some four miles from Waterhouses, Grindon had a goods siding to the east and the usual low passenger platform to the west. The siding was, in effect, a loop that could be shunted from either end – although an intervening section of standard gauge track meant that through running could not take place.

The tiny wooden station building was similar to those found elsewhere on the Leek & Manifold line. A small gable-roofed structure, it stood on a concrete ground sill, and was clad in horizontal weather boarding below waist level; the upper part of the building had prominent external timber framing, the intervening spaces being filled with vertical match boarding. Windows were provided in each end and there were two more in the front wall, on either side of the centrally-placed doorway. The roof was swept down over the platform frontage to form a small canopy, and the end gables sported miniature finials.

Thor's Cave

Departing from Grindon, northbound trains ascended at 1 in 122. The scenery on this section was particularly attractive, and discerning travellers were treated to many tantalising views as their trains meandered through a deep wooded gorge. The gradient steepened, at one point, to 1 in 66, but this soon eased to 1 in 1650 as the winding single line followed the River Manifold upstream towards Thor's Cave.

Serving a popular tourist spot, Thor's Cave (for Wetton) was 4¾ miles from Waterhouses. The single platform was sited on the east side of the line, and the wooden station building resembled that at neighbouring Grindon. Nearby, a somewhat larger wooden structure had (until its removal in 1917) provided food and liquid refreshments for thirsty summer travellers, but no goods facilities were available here, the station being intended primarily for tourists.

Thor's cave itself was situated to the south of the railway, and this spectacular natural feature was always a highly-popular attraction for visiting tourists; the cave was privately-owned, a small charge being levied before visitors could enter the 60 ft high cavern. Thor's Cave station was about one mile from Wetton village and, in the days before motor transport, the inhabitants of this remote place may have enjoyed their scenic walk to the railway.

Grindon station looking south towards Waterhouses after closure, on 3rd May, 1934. The goods siding was arranged as a 'loop', the centre portion being occupied by a length of standard gauge track with room for about two wagons.   *H.C. Casserley*

A typical view along the line near Grindon on 3rd May, 1934.   *H.C. Casserley*

Thor's Cave station seen from Thor's Cave itself on 3rd May, 1934; the stony bed of the River Manifold can be seen beside the railway. *H.C. Casserley*

A useful portrait of Thor's Cave station (looking north). Note that no platform lighting was ever provided at the intermediate stations; the earth closet can be seen behind the simple station building. *H.C. Casserley*

Redhurst Crossing Halt, looking south on 3rd May, 1934; the milk platform is in the distance. Note the grounded coach body to the right and the scalloped nameboard behind the platform. *H.C. Casserley*

A 2-coach train at Wetton Mill station around 1930; the extended coal bunker on the engine can be clearly seen. *J.R. Morten*

Wetton Mill after closure on 3rd May, 1934. The station is intact apart from the removal of the platform seats. *H.C. Casserley*

Another view of Wetton Mill, looking north in the direction of Hulme End. The overgrown sidings suggest that little goods traffic can have been handled there for several years. *Lens of Sutton*

Courtesy J.M. Strange

Two commercial postcard
portraying the beauty and tran
quility of Wetton Mill.
Oakwood Collectio

Redhurst Crossing Halt

Still following the river, the route climbed northwards from Thor's Cave on a 1 in 130 rising gradient. Redhurst, the next stopping place, was 5¼ miles from Waterhouses; no goods facilities were available, but the halt nevertheless provided a convenient place for the loading and unloading of milk churns. Here, the railway crossed the River Manifold on a two-span steel girder bridge supported by substantial stone piers; of similar design to the other Leek & Manifold bridges, this simple structure incorporated light-weight metal walkways on either side of the track. There were no parapets, and the permanent way was laid directly onto the bridge girders.

Redhurst Crossing Halt did not appear in the timetables until 1915–16, and, as mentioned in Chapter One, it was treated as a request stop. An old coach body functioned as a makeshift waiting shed for people wishing to use the halt, and the name REDHURST CROSSING was displayed on a charac-teristic Leek & Manifold scalloped nameboard.

Wetton Mill

Still climbing steadily at 1 in 130, the sinuous narrow gauge line ran north-westwards for about 10 chains (⅛ mile), and trains then crossed the River Manifold on another girder bridge – the twelfth river crossing since leaving Waterhouses. At this point the valley became less gorge-like, but the surrounding scenery lost none of its romantic quality, and appreciative travellers were treated to many fine views as their trains glided smoothly along behind the bustling 2–6–4T locomotives.

Northwards, the line continued towards Wetton Mill, crossing a tributary of the Manifold on another girder bridge and then passing over a minor road on the level. One of the more 'important' intermediate stations, Wetton Mill possessed a loop siding and a dead-end spur ending in the usual section of standard gauge track. A standard Leek & Manifold wooden building was provided, and minor details included a couple of wooden seats and an ornate nameboard with scalloped ends.

Wetton Mill itself – the subject of many Edwardian picture postcards – was only a short distance from the railway, while Wetton Mill Bridge was a noted local beauty spot; there was always water here, although in summer-time the Manifold was often dry below Darfur Crags (between Thor's Cave and Wetton Mill).

Butterton

Having left Wetton Mill, northbound trains faced gradients of 1 in 50, 1 in 110 and 1 in 200, followed immediately by another short stretch of 1 in 50. Beyond, the line dipped at 1 in 434 as it passed through Swainsley tunnel; this, the only tunnel on the line, was said to have been built at the insistence of Sir Thomas Wardle who did not want the view from nearby Swainsley Hall to be spoiled. The tunnel was 164 yards long, but as the Leek & Manifold was designed to accommodate full-sized wagons on its ingenious transporter wagons the bore was no less than 15 ft 3 in. high! The tunnel was

Butterton station, looking east towards Swainsley Hall – the residence of Leek and Manifold Director Sir Thomas Wardle. The characteristic L&MR transhipment siding is clearly visible in the foreground. *Lens of Sutton*

A further photograph in the series taken by Mr Casserley after the closure of the line, on 3rd May, 1934. This view of Butterton is looking south: standard gauge siding to the left and the typical Leek & Manifold waiting shelter to the right. *H.C. Casserley*

lined with a double ring of brickwork and its simple arched portals were faced with stone – the north portal having a high parapet while the south entrance was more or less devoid of detail.

Emerging into daylight once more, trains ran a short distance to Butterton – a wayside stopping place with a single siding and typical Leek & Manifold station building; the passenger platform was on the left hand of the line, and the station was 6¾ miles from Waterhouses.

Butterton's track layout was simple in the extreme, with just one turnout giving access to the single siding goods yard; the siding, which faced towards Hulme End, could be shunted only by northbound trains. The points were released by an Annett's key, and trap points at the north end of the siding prevented runaway wagons from fouling the main line. A short length of 4 ft 8½ in. gauge track allowed standard gauge wagons to be accommodated in the goods yard, but there were no cattle pens, coal wharves or other goods facilities. As usual on the Leek & Manifold line, the standard gauge spur was laid with 35 lb. per yard flat-bottomed rail – this being sufficient to support individual wagons (though in normal circumstances 35 lb. rail would have been too weak for main line usage).

Ecton for Warslow

From Butterton the route meandered north-eastwards as it pursued its circuitous course towards Hulme End. The railway was cut into a ledge in the side of the valley, the river being on the right hand side of the line for much of the distance between Butterton and Ecton. Nearing Ecton for Warslow the line crossed to the opposite bank of the river, and with Ecton Hill rising to 1,211 ft on the right hand side trains reached Ecton, the penultimate station (7¼ miles).

As we have seen, Ecton was once a busy mining and quarrying centre, but the railway came too late to save the local copper mines and no mining revival ever took place. In the 1920s, however, the opening of a milk factory at last provided a reliable source of bulk freight traffic for the line, and thereafter standard gauge milk tanks were regularly transported to and from Ecton.

Ecton boasted a relatively complex track layout incorporating a loop and two dead-end sidings, one of which served a standard gauge loading dock while the other diverged southwards to reach the nearby milk factory (built on the site of a former copper smelter). In earlier days, the layout had consisted of a single loop siding with a central standard gauge section, and substantial alterations had been necessary when the creamery siding and associated loop line was installed.

Ecton's station building was another Leek & Manifold-style wooden waiting shed resembling those found elsewhere on the line; a minor road crossed the line on the level at the north end of the 6 inch high passenger platform, but there were few other features of interest. The station was surrounded by spoil heaps and other relics of the mining industry, and in this context it is interesting to record that waste material from these abandoned workings was used as ballast during the construction of the railway in 1902–04; the stone was crushed on site, and surplus ballast was sold to local farmers at 4d. per ton.

Top The south portal of Swainsley tunnel which carried the line under part of the Swainsley estate. Note the LMS bridge plate; 3rd May, 1934.   *H.C. Casserley*

Middle A view from a northbound train (the 11.40 am from Waterhouses) approaching Swainsley tunnel on 29th April, 1933.
                                        H.C. Casserley

Right An unusual view taken inside the 164 yds-long brick-lined tunnel after closure. The bore was 12 ft wide and 15 ft 3 in. high, the radius of the arch being 7 ft 1½ in.
                                        H.C. Casserley

Ecton station looking north in the early days. The tiny wooden waiting room cost £40 when it was erected in 1904.

Lens of Sutton

A later view of Ecton, taken after closure, 3rd May, 1934.

H.C. Casserley

A fine view of *J.B. Earle* at Hulme End, this time on 29th April, 1933.   *H.C. Casserley*

Hulme End looking towards Waterhouses just after closure on 3rd May, 1934.
H.C. Casserley

Hulme End

Departing from Ecton, northbound trains crossed the minor road to Warslow village on the level and then passed through a shallow cutting before crossing the River Manifold for the last time. Curving north-eastwards the route climbed gently on a 1 in 297 rising gradient, although the ascent steepened to 1 in 73 on the final approach to Hulme End. With their destination now in site, trains slowed for the last few hundred yards into Hulme End station, and here, some 45 minutes after leaving Waterhouses, the 8¾ mile journey came to an end.

Hulme End (for Hartington) was the most substantial station on the Leek & Manifold line. The facilities provided included a lengthy platform which, like others on the Manifold line, was about 6 inches high. There was a run-round loop on one side of the platform, and two goods sidings on the other; the sidings incorporated lengths of standard gauge track for use in conjunction with the railway's transporter wagons, and further sidings fanned out from the run-round loop to serve an engine shed and carriage shed.

The station building at Hulme End was larger than those found elsewhere on the line, though it was of similar design to the others in that its upper part sported external timber framing with intervening match boarding. The lower part of the main exterior walls was formed of lapped weather boards, these being laid horizontally while the match boarding was vertical. This wooden building stood on a brick ground sill, and its pitched roof was swept down over the platform frontage to form a projecting canopy. Internally the building contained a booking office as well as waiting room facilities – Hulme End being the only Leek & Manifold station (apart from Waterhouses) to issue tickets on a regular basis. There was a brick chimney stack at one end of the building, and a stovepipe chimney projected skywards at the opposite end of the structure.

The earliest livery details are unclear, but photographic evidence suggests that an elaborate colour scheme was originally employed; the predominant colour was probably creamish-buff, but the external timber framing was picked out in a much darker colour which (by analogy with other railway colour schemes) was probably brown. Barge boards and window frames seem to have been white, though in later years the entire structure was painted overall in a dark (probably brown) colour scheme.

The engine shed was a two-road structure with an arc roof, the main construction material being corrugated iron. Locomotives entered the shed through wooden doors in the west wall, and a low clerestory facilitated smoke emission; there were, in addition, four tall smoke vents which were probably linked to a smoke trough above the two shed roads.

The adjacent carriage shed was similar to the engine shed, albeit without the clerestory or smoke vents; the main construction material was again corrugated iron. Other buildings at Hulme End included a tall (but very slim) water tower and a variety of small huts, stores and sheds. A raised timber coaling stage was sited near the water tank, and one of the engine shed roads was spanned by a moving gantry for use during locomotive repair operations. Engines were able to take water by means of a flexible hose

A very early view of Hulme End on the opening day; the standard gauge sidings have not yet been laid and the carriage shed (*right*) appears

attached to the side of the water tank, or from a simple hydrant type water column at the very end of the line. The water was supplied from a spring in the surrounding hills, an overshot water wheel being employed to drive a pump which, in turn, lifted the water to the raised tank.

Although the Leek & Manifold line was a simple system with no more than two locomotives, Hulme End was equipped with rudimentary signalling facilities consisting of red home and starting semaphore arms mounted on a single post at the station throat. There was no signal box, but an open 5-lever frame was strategically-sited near the end of the platform.

Minor details at Hulme End were of a varied nature. There was, for example, an old short-wheelbase coach body beside the main station building – this was used for the storage of bicycles, small parcels and similar items. A similar grounded coach body was positioned near the carriage sidings and this ancient vehicle functioned as a tool shed for the permanent way department. Other small sheds were used as offices by local coal merchants, and there was a gentlemen's urinal at the very end of the ground level platform.

One of the company's 12 platform seats was positioned in front of the station building, in which position the canopy afforded a modicum of shelter during wet weather. In earlier years, around 1905, there had been another seat on the platform, but this was apparently removed at an early date – possibly for use at one of the smaller intermediate stations.

At night, the platform was illuminated by oil lamps mounted in simple glass lanterns; these were bolted to the front of the station building or attached to upright timber posts on the platform. A peculiarity of the station which may be mentioned was its loading gauges; one of these was logically positioned in the goods yard, but the other was sited beside the carriage sidings – where it fulfilled no obvious function because these sidings were not used for loading or unloading.

Hulme End itself was merely a hamlet, the nearest 'town' being Hartington, some two miles to the east. There was very little for visiting tourists to see at Hulme End, the only buildings being some scattered cottages and the aptly-named 'Light Railway Hotel'. Perhaps optimistically, the L&MVLR terminus was officially called 'Hulme End for Sheen & Hartington', and this cumbersome name was displayed in full on the station nameboard.

In reality, Hartington was only 1½ miles from Hartington station on the LNWR Ashbourne to Buxton line, and most local residents regarded the North Western line as their primary rail link to the outside world; the Leek & Manifold route was seen as little more than a 'toy' railway, although the inhabitants of Hulme End and the immediate vicinity relied on the L&MVLR to bring modest quantities of coal, animal feed and general merchandise into the area. Another regular flow of traffic was beer for consumption in the Light Railway Hotel (and possibly other local public houses); this traffic had been carried on the L&MVLR for many years, and the Leek & Manifold minute books record that, shortly after opening, the Directors considered the provision of 'extra cellarage' at Hulme End for use in connection with beer traffic.

It is interesting to reflect that, if original plans had come to fruition, Hulme End would have become a through station on an extended Leek & Manifold system stretching for some 20 miles from Waterhouses to the fashionable inland resort of Buxton. As we have seen, the idea of a Buxton extension was under consideration during the early 1900s, and a possible route was actually surveyed by Mr Calthrop. The Directors had always anticipated that the extension would be built – for only then would the Manifold line be able to tap an area of significant population. If implemented in its entirety the Buxton extension scheme would have ensured a ready supply of summer tourist traffic – and the Leek & Manifold line might then have stood a better chance of survival during the bleak years of the depression. Sadly, the big main line companies were reluctant to let the Manifold line compete for their own Buxton traffic and this, together with opposition from landowners, meant that the Leek & Manifold route was destined to end in the middle of a field at Hulme End until its premature demise in March 1934.

WATERHOUSES STATION.

The standard gauge station at Waterhouses in 1905; a North Staffordshire Railway class 'B' 2–4–0T stands in the single platform with an inspection saloon. The Leek & Manifold waiting shelter is prominent to the left of the picture.

Chapter Five
Locomotives, Rolling Stock and Other Details

The Leek & Manifold Railway possessed just two locomotives throughout its life, and as we have seen these were built by Messrs Kitson & Co in 1904. The engines, both 2−6−4Ts, arrived in April 1904, and they became L&MR Nos. 1 and 2, *E.R. Calthrop* and *J.B. Earle* respectively. The locomotives were of identical design and appearance, and their contract price was £1,725 (per engine). Their basic dimensions were as follows:

Cylinders (outside)	11½ in. × 16 in.
Driving wheels	2 ft 6 in. diameter
Leading wheels	1 ft 11 in. diameter
Trailing wheels	1 ft 11 in. diameter
Heating surface	405 sq. ft
Grate area	10 sq. ft
Boiler pressure	160 lb. per square inch
Water capacity	600 gallons
Coal capacity	1 ton
Length	26 ft 3 in.
Length overall	29 ft 2 in.
Coupled wheelbase	6 ft
Total wheelbase	20 ft 6 in.
Boiler diameter	2 ft 11½ in.
Maximum height	9 ft 10 in.
Weight	26 tons 16 cwt.
Tractive effort	9,790 lb.

Externally, the two engines were handsome machines, their running plates, side tanks and boiler fittings being well-proportioned in relation to their 29 ft overall length. The side tanks were partially cut-away to permit easy access to the motion, and the engines were equipped with large and commodious cabs. When first delivered the locomotives were painted in a chocolate brown livery with white (or possibly cream) lining; later, they carried North Staffordshire red livery with yellow lining on the side tanks, bunkers and buffer beams.

Both engines sported huge headlamps and this gave them a faintly 'colonial' appearance – indeed, they were remarkably similar to the class of 0−8−4 tank engines that E.R. Calthrop had earlier designed for the Barsi Railway in India; these had also been built by Kitsons, and it is possible that the export design were adapted for use on the Leek & Manifold line.

Small modifications took place from time to time, one of the first changes being the removal of the original hooters (ordinary whistles were fitted instead). A subsequent modification concerned the coal bunkers, which received extra side sheeting in order to increase their coal capacity. Ramsbottom safety valves were initially carried on the domes, but these were later replaced by Ross pop safety valves.

The locomotives usually ran with their chimneys facing Waterhouses, bunker-first running being the norm between Waterhouses and Hulme End; on one occasion, however, E.R. *Calthrop* arrived back from Stoke (where

heavy repairs were undertaken) facing the 'wrong' way. Double-heading was not unknown, particularly during the summer season when goods vehicles were pressed into service as emergency passenger stock.

Everard Calthrop's work on the Barsi Railway has already been alluded to, but it may be worth adding a little more detail on this subject in order to explain the relationship that existed between the Barsi locomotives and the L&MVLR engines. It is often said that *E.R Calthrop* and *J.B. Earle* were copies of engines already supplied by Kitsons for the Indian line, but this is an over-simplification in that the *original* Barsi locomotives were 0–8–4Ts – albeit of similar appearance to the L&MVLR engines. There can be little doubt that the two Manifold engines were based upon the earlier Barsi tanks, and in this context *The Locomotive Magazine* unambiguously stated the Leek & Manifold 2–6–4Ts were a 'modification of those . . . on the Barsi Light Ry (India) which were built by Messrs Kitson & Co. of Leeds to Mr Calthrop's designs'. However, secondary sources do not make it clear that 12 more Barsi engines were built between 1905 and 1915, and these were virtually copies of the Leek & Manifold engines! In other words, although *E.R. Calthrop* and *J.B. Earle* were based upon the original Barsi 0–8–4Ts, they were themselves the prototypes for further Indian locomotives. Moreover, the Leek & Manifold/Barsi design was so successful that in 1915 two similar engines were ordered from Kitsons for work on the Evrykhou extension of the 2 ft 6 in. gauge Cyprus Government Railway; two more of the same general type were delivered to the Cyprus line in 1920.

An attractive view of locomotive No. 2 *J.B. Earle* leaving Butterton in LMS days; note the substantially-constructed bridge and the LMS bridge plate.   *E.R. Morten*

An impressive broadside view of locomotive No.
J.B. Earle at Hulme End on 29th April, 1933; note th
outside counterweights on the driving wheels.
H.C. Casserle

Detail of J.B. Earle's nameplate.   H.C. Casserl

Another side view of J.B. Earle in the LMS era. Th
headlamps were not used – at least not in the 192
or 1930s.   E.R. Morte

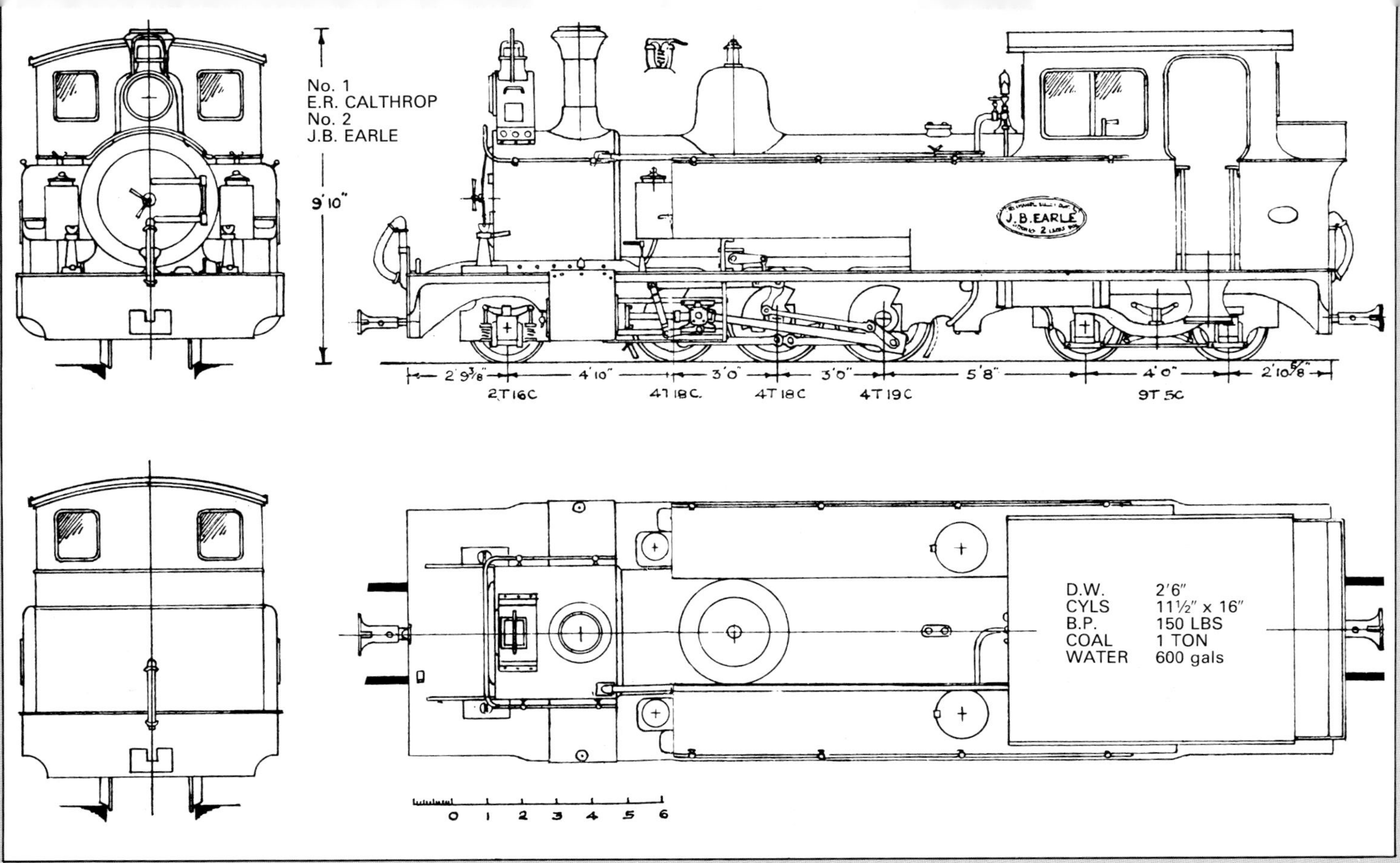

No. 1 E.R. CALTHROP
No. 2 J.B. EARLE

J.B. EARLE

9'10"

2'0"8"
2'10"8"
9T 5c
4'0"
5'8"
4T 19C
3'0"
4T 18C
3'0"
4T 18C
4'10"
2'3⅝"
2T 16C

D.W.   2'6"
CYLS   11½" x 16"
B.P.   150 LBS
COAL   1 TON
WATER   600 gals

0 1 2 3 4 5 6

Leek & Manifold Valley Light Rly 3rd class cars Nos 2 & 4 (LMS 14991 & 14992) Tare 12.14.0, 40 seats drawn by R.E. Tustin.
Courtesy Model Railway News

The links between the Leek & Manifold Railway and these other 2 ft 6 in. gauge lines are of great interest, but should not be over-stated. The Barsi and Cyprus Government engines were, for example, somewhat bigger than the L&MVLR prototypes, with a weight of 36 tons and a tractive effort of 13,790 lb. They were also much longer than the Manifold tanks, with a much greater gap between their coupled wheels and trailing bogies (i.e. to provide sufficient room for their fireboxes and ash pans). In outward appearance the 16 colonial engines closely resembled their smaller sisters on the Leek & Manifold line, cabs, boiler fittings, headlamps and other details being of identical design. Some useful comparative data is given in *Table 1* (below):

Table 1

Comparative Dimensions of the Leek & Manifold, Barsi and Cyprus Locomotives

	Leek & Manifold	Barsi Light Rly	Cyprus Govt Rly
Type	2−6−4 tank	4−8−4 tank	4−8−4 tank
Gauge	2 ft 6 in.	2 ft 6 in.	2 ft 6 in.
Date built	1904	1905, 1907, 1915	1915, 1920
Total	2 engines	12 engines	4 engines
Cylinders	11½ in. × 16 in.	13 in. × 18 in.	13 in. × 18 in.
Coupled wheels	2 ft 6 in.	2 ft 6 in.	2 ft 6 in.
Boiler pressure	160 psi	160 psi	160 psi
Tractive effort	9,790 lb.	13,790 lb.	13,790 lb.
Grate area	10 sq. ft	10.6 sq. ft	10.6 sq. ft.
Solid fuel	1 ton	1.75 tons	1.75 tons
Water capacity	600 gallons	920 gallons	920 gallons
Coupled wheelbase	6 ft	8.25 ft	8.25 ft
Total wheelbase	20.5 ft	26.25 ft	26.25 ft
Weight (total)	26 tons 16 cwt	36 tons	36 tons

It will be seen that there were numerous similarities between the Leek & Manifold engines and their overseas counterparts, and it seems that the L&MVLR locomotives and the export machines utilised many common components. The large, tropical-style cabs, for instance, were common to the Barsi, Cyprus and L&MVLR engines, while the domes, chimneys and safety valves were of identical appearance. All of these Kitson-built engines were inside-framed, a particularly distinctive common feature being the use of *outside* balance weights that were attached to the axle ends – these heavy metal castings being entirely separate from the coupled wheels.

Writing in 1955, the anonymous authors of *The Leek & Manifold Valley Light Railway* noted that E.R. Calthrop and J.B. Earle were originally fitted with an attachment at the rear of the cabs so that large colonial-style headlamps could be carried for use when running bunker-first, while both engines had holes in their buffer beams to accommodate cow catchers. Such fittings were never carried on the Leek & Manifold, but the export models were equipped with cow catchers and rear headlamps from their inception.

The two Leek & Manifold engines performed well in everyday service, but like all steam locomotives they exhibited certain idiosyncrasies – notably an

Locomotive No. 1 *E.R. Calthrop* stands beneath the travelling gantry outside the sheds at Hulme End. Although Leek & Manifold engines usually ran with their chimneys facing Waterhouses, No. 1 is here facing the opposite direction.   *Lens of Sutton*

Photographs of locomotive No. 1 *E.R. Calthrop* are comparatively rare, perhaps because the engine saw less use than No. 2 *J.B. Earle*. Here the engine stands outside the engine shed at Hulme End with No. 2 coupled at the rear; No. 1 is still facing towards Hulme End, 29th April, 1933.   *H.C. Casserley*

alleged tendency to work best when running bunker-first towards Hulme
End. One assumes that this phenomenon was associated with adhesion on
the long climb up to the terminus – when running bunker-first the water in
the side tanks must have been concentrated over the coupled wheels, in
which position it would have added additional weight where it was most
needed (especially on the 1 in 50 ascent towards Swainsley Tunnel). What-
ever the reason, the engines were, for many years, worked bunker-first
towards the upper terminus, and when E.R. Calthrop was returned from
overhaul facing the 'wrong' way local railwaymen made frantic efforts to
turn the engine round with the aid of jacks.[27] These efforts were futile, and
thereafter the engine ran – apparently successfully – facing Hulme End.
Writing in the March 1957 Model Railway Constructor, Mr F. Hackett
suggested that this incident took place during the 1920s, but photographic
evidence indicates that E.R. Calthrop was running the 'wrong' way round in
1933.

   The two L&MVLR locomotives were, for all intents and purposes,
identical, though small differences had been introduced by the 1930s. The
most noticeable difference concerned the domes – E.R. Calthrop having a
shorter, slightly fatter dome in comparison to that carried by J.B. Earle. In its
final years, E.R. Calthrop also sported a tiny handle on the left hand side of
the smoke box door. Both engines originally carried oval maker's plates on
either side of the bunkers, but J.B. Earle's plate was removed during the LMS
era, and in its place the engine carried a circular LMS crest; it is believed
that, for a short time, one of the engines ran in LMS red livery while its
companion was painted unlined black – though this assertion is hard to
prove without the firm evidence of colour photography!

   It would, finally, be appropriate to mention that the two engines incorporated several innovative features that would not have been apparent to the
casual observer. The leading wheels, for example, were fitted with a spring
device to guide the engines round sharp curves and so relieve the excessive
pressure that would otherwise have been put on the leading coupled wheels.
As an extra precaution, there was also a simple pipe system whereby water
could be used to lubricate the flanges – although this particular innovation
tended to induce wheel-slip. Another unusual device enabled train crews to
spray water onto the fire in an emergency, while the patent Jones-Calthrop
couplers were fitted with Calthrop's patent 'radiating gear' to ensure that
they always engaged properly.

   In view of the above-mentioned special features it comes as something of a
surprise to discover that the prominent headlamps were acetylene rather
than electric. On the other hand there is a general concensus of opinion that
the lamps were never used in ordinary service, and a dynamo system would
clearly have been superfluous!

Passenger Vehicles

   Turning now to the railway's passenger rolling stock, it comes as no
surprise to discover that E.R. Calthrop once again drew heavily on his
experience in India when drawing-up plans for the Leek & Manifold

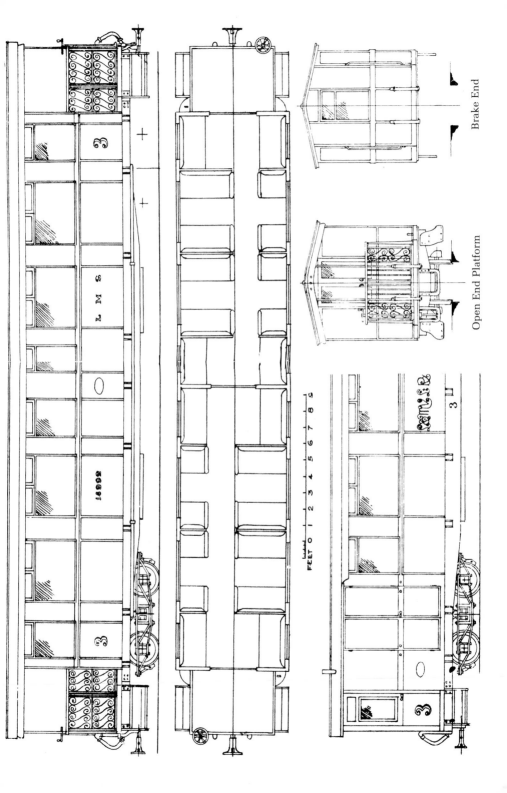

Brake End

Open End Platform

FEET 0 1 2 3 4 5 6 7 8 9

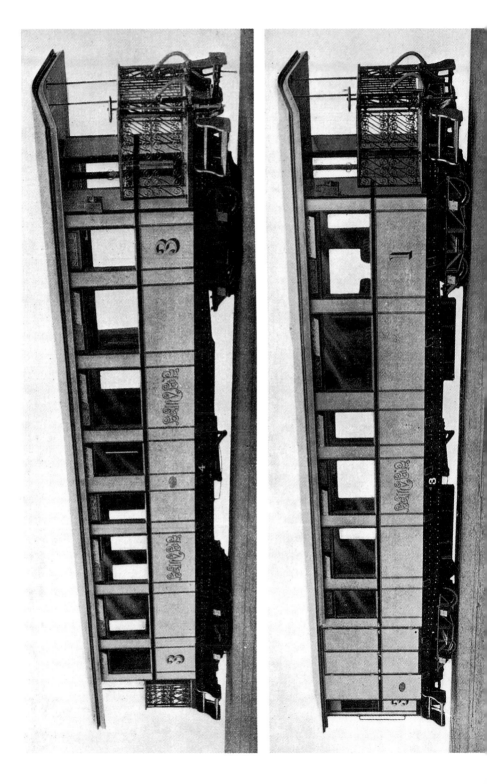

passenger vehicles. 'In designing the rolling stock', explained *The Railway Magazine*, 'Mr Calthrop followed the lines, subject to improvements suggested by later experience, of the stock designed . . . for the Barsi Light Railway of India, the construction and equipment of which were carried out entirely from his plans'.[28] The result was a small fleet of innovative bogie coaches that were, by English narrow gauge standards, of immense proportions.

The L&MVLR coaches were certainly long, but the boldest feature of their design was not the 42 ft length but the decision to put an 8 ft wide vehicle on 2 ft 6 in. gauge bogies! This was, in 1904, a controversial decision, and *The Railway Magazine* noted that 'special sanction was obtained from the Board of Trade' before vehicles of 'the dimensions desired' could be put into public service. However, many commentators applauded Mr Calthrop for demonstrating how existing technology could be pushed to the limit, and in this respect the Leek & Manifold Valley Light Railway was widely seen as a viable demonstration of what could be achieved on even the smallest of gauges.

The four tramway-type bogie vehicles delivered in 1904 comprised the total carriage fleet of the Leek & Manifold Railway. Built by the Electric Railway & Tramway Carriage Works of Preston, they were of two types, two being brake composites while the remaining vehicles were ordinary thirds. Each coach was 42 ft long, 8 ft wide and 10 ft high, access to the interior saloons being by means of colonial-type end platforms. The third class coaches had platforms at each end, but the brake composites had open verandahs at one end only – the other end being occupied by the guard's compartment (through which third class passengers reached their seats).

Internally, the thirds were divided into two open saloons by a transverse bulkhead; each saloon held 20 passengers, the total seating capacity being 40 people. The seats were upholstered, and large windows enabled travellers to admire the passing scenery as their trains ambled along the picturesque Manifold line. Most of the seats were arranged on a 2 + 1 pattern, but there was a limited number of longitudinal seats in each vehicle. Total weight of the thirds was 12 tons 14 cwt.

The L&MR brake composites also contained two open saloons, the first class sections having accommodation for 8 passengers while the slightly larger third class portions (next to the guard) could hold 20 people. The first class seats were very comfortably padded, and each traveller sat in an individual 'armchair' type seat. All of the Leek & Manifold coaches were lit by electricity, and there was provision for smokers and non-smokers.

Many further details of the coaches appeared in an article published by *The Engineer* on 21st October, 1904, and this article (which was written after the Leek & Manifold Valley Railway had been in operation throughout its first busy summer season) is worth quoting in some detail. The article suggested that 'practical men' had hitherto regarded narrow gauge railways 'as being little better than toys, both on account of their diminutive rolling stock and by reason of the great expense and delay involved in the transhipment of goods at any junction with a standard gauge concern'. However, the Leek & Manifold Valley Railway had shown that such railways could

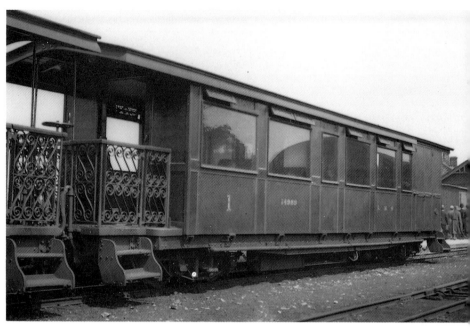

One of the two Leek & Manifold brake composites; the vehicle is in LMS red livery and carries the number 14989. The location is Hulme End.   *Photomatic Ltd*

Coaches Nos. 14991 and 14989 in the platform line at Hulme End after closure, on 3rd May, 1934. Two vacuum pipes were needed because the transporter cars had a very short hose that would not easily have reached a single hose on the coaches. *Unfortunately this photograph is damaged on the right hand edge.*   *H.C. Casserley*

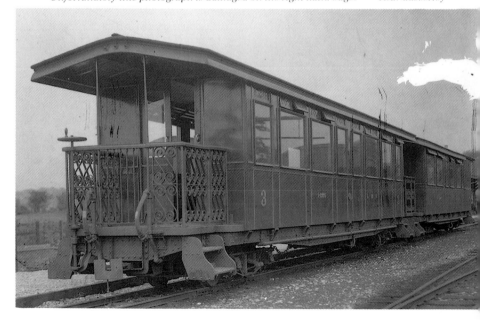

'attract a very large tourist and holiday traffic', and its large bogie coaches had frequently 'carried over eighty passengers each'. The L&MVLR vehicles were described as follows:

> The coaches were constructed by the Electric Railway and Tramway Carriage Works Limited, of Preston, to the designs of Mr E.R. Calthrop, M.Inst.C.E., of 3 Crosby Square London E.C., who has had an opportunity in the carrying out of the Leek & Manifold Railway of demonstrating in this country the capacity of his 2 ft 6 in.gauge rolling stock which, we understand, has proved itself so successful in India.
>
> The underframes are constructed of plate and angle irons, and were tested with 20 tons deadweight before being placed under the coach bodies, under which they showed no appreciable deflection. The bogies are . . . of the diamond-frame swing-bolster types fitted with double laminated springs. The wheels are of chilled cast iron, and were manufactured by the British Griffen Chilled Iron and Steel Company of Barrow-in-Furness. The central buffers are made in accordance with Jones and Calthrop's patents, and are fitted with Calthrop's patented radiating gear, which is a mechanism operated by the bogie, and so arranged to move the loose uncoupled buffer into such a position that it will always couple with another vehicle irrespective of differences in their length, or of whether the vehicles are on a straight line or a curve of any radius.
>
> The whole of the rolling stock is fitted with the Automatic Vacuum Brake Company's vacuum brake, and the coaches are fitted with Stone's system of electric light . . . To engineers only accustomed to the small stock ordinarily in use on narrow gauge railways, these coaches appear to be extremely large for a 2 ft 6 in. gauge, but it is claimed that their safety is beyond dispute, and that any doubts as to stability are immediately dispelled upon riding in them. They are said to travel perfectly smoothly without the slightest roll, although the railway consists almost entirely of curves, some of which are of so small a radius as 4 chains, or 26 ft, and an average speed of 30 miles per hour has been obtained over the whole line.[29]

Locomotive *J.B. Earle* rounds a tight curve near Waterhouses on 28th June, 1933. Leek and Manifold covered van (No. 2) is marshalled immediately behind the engine.

H.C. Casserley

Above shows the interior of the Third Class coach and *below*, the First Class.
Courtesy The Engineer

The article also contained a very full list of dimensions, and for complete-
ness this additional data is printed below; it will be seen that the maximum
length of each vehicle was 45 ft, although 42 ft is usually quoted as the
nominal length of the coaches between the bulkheads. On a very minor
point, one might add that the maximum internal height of 7 ft between floor
level and the under side of the roof was generous enough to accommodate an
Edwardian gentleman in a top hat (although one hopes that a real gentleman
would have removed his head gear before entering the vehicle)! The
principal dimensions of the four L&MVLR coaches were as follows:

	ft	in.
Gauge	2	6
Length over buffers	45	0
Centre to centre of bogie	28	0
Rigid wheelbase of each bogie	4	3
Diameter of wheels	1	11
Height above buffer centre above rail when loaded	1	2
Length of roof	43	6
Height of roof from rail level	9	9
Extreme width (over roof)	8	0
Clear width inside saloons	6	9
Height from floor to under side of roof	7	1³/₈
Clear headroom under lowest arch rail	6	3
Width of first class seats	2	2
Width of third class seats	1	3
Height of windows	2	6
Length of first class plate glass windows	4	8
Length of third class plate glass windows	3	10

Unusually, the four L&MR coaches had pitched roofs instead of the more
familiar elliptical or clerestory variety. Livery was bright yellow, with black
ironwork; the letters 'L&MVLR' were displayed in curious intertwined
lettering. Later, the attractive yellow livery was abandoned and in its place
the coaches carried North Staffordshire Railway dark red livery. In LMS
days the livery was maroon with yellow and black lining, the initials 'LMS'
being displayed in shaded lettering.

The coaches were equipped with American-style hand-brake wheels on
their end platforms, and there were also two sets of vacuum brake pipes at
each end. This unusually-generous provision enabled the passenger
vehicles to be coupled to the transporter cars (which had very short vacuum
brake connections on one side only). When marshalling trains containing
one or more transporters railway staff connected whichever brake hose was
most convenient and left the other unattached – it should perhaps be added
that the sharp curves on the Manifold line created special problems in
relation to the overhang at each end of the 42 ft coaches, and in this respect
the positioning of the vacuum hoses was a critical factor in rolling stock
design.

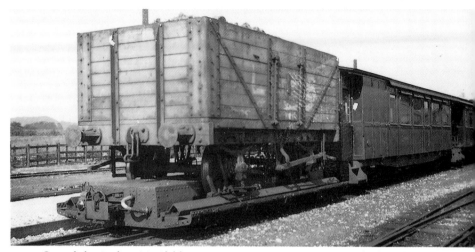

One of the Leek & Manifold transporter wagons conveying a 7-plank coal wagon from Waterhouses. The train has just arrived at Hulme End; note the short vacuum pipe connection on the transporter wagon.   *Lens of Sutton*

A transporter wagon with NSR wagon No. 2949 awaiting its train at Hulme End.
National Railway Museum

An end-on view of transporter car No. 19538 at Hulme End on 29th April, 1933. The wheel clamps are clearly visible.   *H.C. Casserley*

The Transporter Wagons

The Leek & Manifold Railway owned very few freight vehicles , the idea being that coal and other heavy consignments would be carried in standard gauge wagons. It follows from this that the narrow gauge transporter wagons were of particular importance in relation to Leek & Manifold freight operations, and it would be useful to examine these distinctive vehicles in some detail.

There were five transporter wagons in all, two being supplied by the Cravens Railway Carriage & Wagon Co. in 1904, followed by a further pair in 1907–8; a fifth transporter – of different design – was built at Stoke Works after the 1923 amalgamation. The contract price for the first two wagons was £449, and these unusual vehicles had the following basic dimensions:

	ft	in.
Gauge	2	6
Length	19	6
Width overall	8	0
Rigid wheelbase of each bogie	4	3
Diameter of wheels	1	9
Distance between bogie centres	9	0
Height of standard gauge rail above track	0	10

The transporter wagons had a tare weight of 4 tons 15 cwt., and could carry a load of 20 tons. They were described as follows by *The Railway Magazine*:

Calthrop's patent transportation car . . . is a novel feature of this railway, and the general introduction of such vehicles should have a considerable effect on the extension of narrow gauge lines, by removing the strongest objection to their use as feeders to railways of the standard gauge. The car is designed for the transport of vehicles of the normal gauge over narrow gauge lines, to avoid the transhipment of the load. From the sides of the car, which has been left as low as possible, two platforms extend, each about 16 inches wide; where these platforms join the edges of the car two slots, formed of a shallow inverted channel iron, serve as rails to receive the wheels of vehicles of the standard gauge. These rails are only 10 inches above the narrow gauge rails. The vehicle to be loaded is pushed against a specially constructed stop block, the transportation car is secured firmly in its position by pulling over a lever, the vehicle is then pushed on to the car, the lever released, and the car is ready to set out on its travels, bearing its big neighbour quite easily and safely.[30]

In practice, a standard gauge wagon could be loaded or unloaded in a matter of minutes, and when secured in position by a system of adjustable clamps the standard gauge vehicle was perfectly safe on its 2 ft 6 in. gauge host vehicle. The system was both simple and ingenious, though few other railways ever made use of Calthrop type transporters. Significantly, the system was employed on at least one other railway – the line in question being the Barsi Light Railway; curiously, the Indian line did not order its first transporters until 1906, and thus the Leek & Manifold Railway could claim to have been the first line to operate these unique vehicles in everyday service.

Open wagons Nos. 195317 and 195318 stand in Waterhouses goods yard on 28th June, 1933. Both vehicles are in their passenger-carrying guise, with seating, side rails and canopies in place. *H.C. Casserley*

The two open wagons (then LMS numbers 195317 and 195318) stand at the end of the Leek & Manifold yard at Waterhouses; these vehicles could be adapted for carrying passengers for which short footboards were provided. *Lens of Sutton*

Before describing the other Leek & Manifold freight vehicles it is necessary to add that one of the transporter wagons was subsequently lengthened
from 19 ft 6 in. to 31 ft in order that 6-wheeled milk vans could safely be
carried. This modification was carried out by the NSR at Stoke Works, but
none of the other transporters were lengthened in this way.

Other Freight Stock

The Leek & Manifold Valley Railway owned just three other freight
vehicles, one of which was a bogie goods van while the remaining two were
low sided bogie goods wagons. The two opens were delivered in time for the
opening of the line in July 1904, and as only two passenger vehicles had
been built in time for the opening the bogie opens were pressed into service
as auxiliary passenger vehicles! The opens were built by the Leeds Forge
Company, and they had the following dimensions:

	ft	in.
Length over buffers	28	0
Length of platform	25	0
Rigid wheelbase of bogie	4	3
Diameter of wheels	1	11
Distance between bogie centres	15	6
Width of vehicle platform	7	0
Height of buffer (loaded)	1	2

Further details were provided in *The Engineer* which printed the
following description of the Leek & Manifold open wagons:

> The low-sided goods wagon is almost an exact duplicate of those built by the
> Leeds Forge Company Limited to Mr Calthrop's designs in 1896 for the Barsi Light
> Railway. On that railway, these wagons have been loaded regularly to about
> 16 tons, and have given, we understand, the greatest satisfaction, and, although
> they have been in use under these large loads for seven years, we are informed that
> repairs have been practically nil . . .
> The weight of these wagons is 5½ tons, including vacuum brake gear, and
> limited to a maximum axle load of 5 tons, they carry a load of 14½ tons on a floor
> area of 175 square feet.[31]

Like all Leek & Manifold freight vehicles, the bogie opens were painted in
the North Staffordshire Railway's dark reddish-brown livery. They were
fitted with standard Leek & Manifold pattern centre buffer/couplings, and
equipped with both vacuum and hand brakes. At the height of the summer
excursion season they were often fitted-up with seats and a system of iron
hoops supporting canvas roofs; in later years they were also fitted with
simple side steps so that elderly (or other less-than-nimble travellers) could
easily climb aboard.

It is, finally, necessary to say a few words about the solitary covered van.
This vehicle was built by the Leeds Forge Company, and its overall dimensions were similar to those of the bogie opens; it ran on 1 ft 11 in. diameter
wheels and the distance between bogie centres was 15 ft 6 in. The van was
25 ft long (excluding the buffer/couplings) and 9 ft 6 in. high. Like so much

else on the Leek & Manifold Railway, the van was of 'colonial' appearance, being similar to the types of modern steel bogie goods vans supplied to railways throughout the British Empire. It was used mainly for the conveyance of milk churns, and its capacity was about 15 tons.

There were, in all, just 12 passenger and freight vehicles in the Leek & Manifold Valley Railway fleet, and a complete stock list is given in *Table 2* (*below*). The fact that no other passenger or freight vehicles were ever provided reflects the paucity of traffic on this somewhat under-utilised light railway – though one might add that, until 1914, the L&MVLR carried around 12,000 excursionists each summer, the bogie open wagons and transporter wagons being used as passenger vehicles if necessary. (The main problem, as far as the Manifold line was concerned, was lack of freight traffic, and it was this factor above all, that ultimately led to the premature closure of the line in 1934.)

Table 2

Summary of Freight and Passenger Rolling Stock on the L&MVLR

Vehicle	Quantity
Brake composite passenger coaches	2
Third class passenger coaches	2
Transporter wagons	5
Open wagons/auxiliary passenger vehicles	2
Bogie goods van	1
Total number of vehicles	12

Railcars on the Manifold Line

The Leek & Manifold Railway was involved in two early railcar experiments, the first of which took place as long ago as 1906 when a Drewry railcar was tested on the railway on behalf of an Indian line. Over two decades later, in July 1932, an Armstrong-Whitworth diesel electric vehicle was tested on the Manifold route prior to shipment to India for use on the 2 ft 6 in. Baroda State Railway.

These trials attracted little publicity, although a photograph showing the Armstrong-Whitworth vehicle at Hulme End appeared in the May 1932 *Railway Magazine*. The railcar had not yet been fitted with seats or bodywork, and it seems that the tests were carried out with the L&MVLR brake composite coach attached as a 'trailer'. The use of diesel power in everyday service would have enabled the Leek & Manifold line to remain in operation for a few more years, but as intimated in Chapter Two the LMS showed no desire to initiate economies that could have prolonged the life of the line, and there was no thought of purchasing railcars for long-term use on the L&MVLR.

Signalling Details

Although there has already been some mention of signalling and single line working there is scope for a more detailed analysis of these aspects of the Leek & Manifold story, and the following details may be useful to modellers (and others) seeking further details of the *minutae* of railway operation.

When first opened the L&MVLR was worked on the one-engine-in-steam system whereby only one engine in steam (or two coupled together) was allowed on the line at any one time. To ensure that only one train *could* leave Hulme End drivers carried a wooden train staff fitted with keys to work the 5-lever ground frame at Hulme End and the points at intermediate stopping places *en route* to Waterhouses. Once the train staff was sent out, there was no means of operating the siding connections at Hulme End, and the other engine was effectively isolated in its shed.

As recounted earlier, it was soon realised that this method of operation was too restrictive; if, for instance, there was shunting to be carried out in the goods yard at Hulme End the spare engine could not be used – while at times of heavy summer traffic it was impossible to send two trains in one direction to cater for special excursion parties or other unexpected demands. To solve this operational problem the NSR introduced the 'train-staff-and-ticket' method of operation which enabled a train to be sent out on the line after the driver had been given a written ticket in lieu of the train staff. The staff itself remained at Hulme End where it could be used to actuate the lever frame so that shunting operations could take place. It was also possible for a second train to be sent out on the line once the first had arrived at Waterhouses – although no train could proceed in the opposite direction until the two trains had entered the lower terminus at Waterhouses.

Documents now held in the Public Record Office at Kew suggest that the Board of Trade sanctioned the introduction of train staff and ticket operation in May 1906, subject, however, to the proviso that trains would not be allowed to pass at the intermediate stations. There is also a reference to operation by 'block telegraph', though it is unclear if this refinement was ever introduced.[32]

Hulme End and Waterhouses stations were linked by telephone, and it was therefore possible for the station master at Hulme End to know when an up train had safely arrived – a following train could then be despatched from the upper terminus with no fear of an end-on collision *en route*. As an added refinement the telephone system could be plugged-in at intermediate points between the upper and lower termini, telephone plugs being available at several of the stations.

Although the loops at Wetton Mill and Ecton were not signalled and could not be used as passing places, the short loop at the eastern end of Water-houses station was equipped with signals for up and down traffic and could (if necessary) have been used as a crossing loop. This facility may indeed have been used for summer Saturday operation after 1906, when, for a few years, the Manifold line was worked on a relatively complex pattern. The 1908 summer timetable examined in Chapter Three would certainly have called for the employment of two trains, and it is likely that the Waterhouses passing loop would have been needed in the event of special excursions or other extra workings being run. In essence the line was, in these years, worked as the following three sections: Hulme End station, Waterhouses station, and the intervening single line section between the loop at Water-houses and the combined home/starter signal at Hulme End.

In later years, the decline in traffic meant that the train staff and ticket system was no longer necessary, and H.C. Casserley recalled that in the LMS period the Manifold line was once again worked on the 'one-engine-in-steam' system. The signals at Waterhouses and Hulme End were however retained, and it was normal for the signal arms to be lowered prior to the arrival or departure of a train. There were, otherwise, just two more fixed signals on the entire line, these being the rotating discs at the Ashbourne Road level crossing; these too were retained until the end of the operation in 1934.

A Note on Other 2 ft 6 in. Gauge Lines

As suggested above the 2 ft 6 in. gauge of the Leek & Manifold Light Railway was somewhat unusual, the 'normal' narrow gauges in the United Kingdom being 2 ft (actually 1 ft 11½ in.) in Wales and 3 ft in Ireland. The choice of 2 ft 6 in. as the gauge of the Leek & Manifold was no doubt a result of this gauge being adopted on the Barsi Railway – though one feels that, (in view of his very strict axle loadings and other specifications) E.R. Calthrop must have had good reasons for selecting this precise width; he probably chose it because 2 ft was considered too narrow for stability at higher speeds, whereas the the wider gauge of 3 ft did not permit sufficient financial savings in a line such as the L&MVLR.

On a footnote, it may be worth mentioning that at least seven other British lines were built to the 2 ft 6 in. gauge; these were the Welshpool & Llanfair Railway, the Alford & Sutton Bridge Tramway, the St Austell & Pentewan Railway, the Sittingbourne & Kemsley line, the Corsham Tramway, and the Chattenden & Upnor Railway. There were, in addition a number of colonial 2 ft 6 in. gauge lines such as the Cyprus Government Railway and of course the Barsi Light Railway. Other overseas systems included the Barbados Light Railway – a 24 mile line linking Bridgetown and St Andrews – and the much larger Sierra Leone Railway from Freetown to Pendembu and Makemis (227 miles). On a smaller scale, there was a 14 mile 2 ft 6 in. gauge line on the island of Mauritius (in addition to the main standard gauge network of about 120 miles).

The Leek & Manifold Line Today

The Manifold line survived as a footpath for several years, and when H.C. Casserley visited the former railway in April 1940 he found that most of the wooden station buildings were still intact, though doors and window glass had been removed. The large wooden nameboards at Thor's Cave, Redhurst Crossing and elsewhere were still in place and, from a distance at least, the abandoned line was recognisable as a former railway.

In 1953 the section of pathway between Redhurst Halt and Butterton was made into a motor road, passing places being installed at intervals so that vehicles could pass each other on the narrow formation. Thereafter, the route was left in three distinct sections, that is to say a pedestrian walkway from Waterhouses to Redhurst Halt, a road from Redhurst to Butterton (including the tunnel) and a further stretch of pathway from Butterton to Hulme End.

Much of the former infrastructure has survived intact. At Waterhouses, the timber goods shed has found a new lease of life as a cycle-hire point, though the nearby passenger station has been demolished. Similarly at Hulme End, the former locomotive shed has survived as part of a council maintenance depot and is still (1988) fully intact and recognisable as a railway building. Perhaps more importantly, the booking office and waiting room has also survived, albeit without its projecting canopy. This is, needless to say, a unique and interesting structure, and one can only hope that this enduring relic of the Leek & Manifold Railway will be properly preserved as one of the last tangible links with the short-lived line.

Elsewhere, many L&MVLR bridges have, of necessity, been maintained in good condition as part of the Manifold footpath, while Wetton Mill delights present-day tourists as an attractively wooded car park and picnic area.

Another visible reminder of the railway can be seen (and even driven through!) at Butterton, where the 12 ft wide brick-lined tunnel is likely to remain for many years as a physical reminder of the L&MVLR. The tunnel entrances still exhude a distinctly 'railway' atmosphere, while the tunnel itself is regarded as an interesting feature on the scenic drive from Redhurst to Butterton.

A Note on Tickets

On a footnote, it may be worth adding that tickets, and other Leek & Manifold memorabilia, occasionally turn up at collector's sales. It is said that the first tickets issued on the line were lettered 'L&MVLR', but most surviving examples would seem to be conventional NSR issues; even these are rare – Hulme End and Waterhouses being the only stations with booking offices. Tickets issued on the trains for journeys to or from intermediate stations seem to have been vertical-type Edmondson cards, though so few tickets have survived that the full story of Leek & Manifold is very hard to elucidate.

References

1. See *The Cromford & High Peak Railway* (Oakwood Press) for further details.
2. Irish Light railway legislation was surprisingly complex, but, generally speaking, earlier legislation such as the Irish Tramways Acts of 1860 and 1861 provided that an Order in Council from the Lord Lieutenant would later be confirmed by an Act of Parliament. This procedure was progressively simplified until, with the English Light Railway Act of 1896, the promoters of lines could proceed with their schemes upon grant of a Light Railway Order – no Act being needed at all.
3. The Light Railways Act 1896.
4. Charles F. Klapper, The Leek & Manifold Section of the LMSR, *The Railway Magazine*, October 1932, p. 253.
5. *Op. cit.* p. 253.
6. PRO Kew RAIL 358/1.
7. Leek & Manifold Valley Light Railway Prospectus 1898.
8. The Leek, Caldon Low & Hartington Light Railways Order 1899.
9. *Ibid.*
10. PRO Kew RAIL 358/1.
11. PRO Kew RAIL 358/1.
12. PRO Kew RAIL 358/1.
13. PRO Kew RAIL 358/1.
14. PRO Kew RAIL 358/1.
15. PRO Kew MT6 1608.
16. Gilbert J. Stoker, Leek & Manifold Railway, *The Railway Magazine* 1904, pp. 213–220.
17. *The Locomotive Magazine* 15th July, 1904, pp. 120–21.
18. PRO Kew RAIL 358/1.
19. PRO Kew RAIL 358/1.
20. PRO MT6 2030/3.
21. See Basil Jeuda, *The Leek, Caldon & Waterhouses Railway* (1980), pp. 24 and 43.
22. H.C. Casserley, The Leek & Manifold Valley Light Railway, *The Railway Magazine*, September–October 1945.
23. W.T.F. Castle, *Model Railway News*, March 1931, pp. 86–87.
24. *The Railway Magazine*, May 1934, pp. 378–79.
25. *The Railway Magazine*, April 1937.
26. *The Railway Magazine*, October 1937.
27. See letter from F. Hackett, *Model Railway Constructor*, March 1957, p. 87.
28. Stoker, *loc. cit.*, *The Railway Magazine*, 1904, p. 217.
29. *The Engineer*, 21st October, 1904, p. 387.
30. Stoker, *loc. cit.*, *The Railway Magazine*, 1904, pp. 218–19.
31. *The Engineer*, 21st October, 1904, p. 387.
32. PRO Kew MT6 2030/3.

Appendix One

Chronological List of Important Dates

1831 Cromford & High Peak Line opened throughout.
1849 Churnet Valley line opened with station at Leek.
1852 NSR branch opened from Rocester to Ashbourne.
1867 NSR direct line from Leek to Stoke opened.
1880 Leek station remodelled.
1894 LNWR opens branch from Buxton to Parsley Hay (1st June).
1895 The Rev. W. Beresford suggests that a Manifold Valley line be made.
1896 Professor John Sheldon calls meeting to discuss the proposal (27th May).
     Light Railways Act passed by Parliament (14th August).
     Rival scheme suggested for Derby–Manchester main line (October).
     Charles Bill meets NSR General Manager to discuss Manifold line.
1897 Light Railway Order applied for (May).
     Public meeting held in Leek Town Hall (2nd July).
     Further meetings held with NSR representatives.
1898 First meeting of L&MVLR Directors held at Leek (21st September).
     Leek & Manifold Light Railway prospectus issued (15th December).
1899 Light Railway Order granted for Leek–Waterhouses–Hulme End line
     (6th March).
     First sod cut at Waterhouses by Earl of Dartmouth (3rd October).
1900 Death of Joseph Forsyth; Everard Calthrop appointed Engineer (December).
1901 Tenders accepted – Hutchinson & Co. to build Leek & Manifold line.
1902 Construction of L&MVLR begins (March).
     Mr Calthrop prepares specifications for engines and rolling stock (May).
     Arrangements made for taking spoil from Ecton (August).
1903 Construction proceeds without incident.
1904 Locomotives delivered.
     Board of Trade inspection of L&MVLR (23rd June).
     Ceremonial opening of Leek & Manifold line (27th June).
     Normal services begin (29th June).
1905 Leek–Waterhouses line opened throughout (1st July).
1906 NSR applies to Board of Trade for permission to alter operating arrangements.
     Extra goods rolling stock ordered.
1909 Death of Sir Thomas Wardle (3rd January).
     Experimental charabanc service between Stoke, Hulme End and Buxton.
1913 Death of Professor Sheldon (23rd August).
1915 Redhurst Crossing Halt officially opened as request stop.
     Death of Charles Bill (9th December); A.J. Hambledon becomes Chairman.
1919 Train services affected by railway strike.
1923 NSR and L&MVLR amalgamated as part of the LMS group.
1926 The General Strike again affects train service.
1932 Ecton creamery closed.
1934 LMS announces that the L&MVLR will be closed (1st March).
     Last trains run between Waterhouses and Hulme End (10th March).
1935 Leek to Waterhouses branch closed to passenger traffic (28th September).
1936 Coaches scrapped at Waterhouses.
1937 L&MVLR engines sold to scrap merchants; lifting completed.
     Trackbed re-opened as a public footpath (23rd July).
1943 Waterhouses station closed to all traffic (1st March).
1953 Redhurst Crossing to Butterton section of L&MVLR opened as road.
1964 Leek to Caldon line closed to goods traffic, remaining open for minerals.

Appendix Two

Facilities at Leek & Manifold Stations

Waterhouses (L&MVLR)
Raised passenger platform
Booking office and waiting room
Signal cabin (also worked NSR line)
Three transhipment sidings
Run-round loop and headshunt
Passing loop
Weigh-house, huts and stores

Sparrowlee for Waterfall
Ground level platform
Old coach body used as waiting shed
Goods siding with 60 ft length of standard
  gauge track
Nameboard and seat

Beeston Tor
Ground level platform
Old coach body used as waiting shed
Refreshment room
Nameboard and seat

Grindon
Ground level platform
Portable Building Co. waiting room
Loop siding incorporating 75 ft standard
  gauge section
Nameboard and seat

Thor's Cave for Wetton
Ground level platform
Portable Building Co. waiting room
Refreshment room (moved 1917)
Nameboard and two seats

Redhurst Crossing Halt
Ground level platform
Old coach body used as waiting room
Milk loading platform
Nameboard and seat

Wetton Mill
Ground level platform
Portable Building Co. waiting room
Loop and dead-end siding with standard
  gauge section
Nameboard and two seats

Butterton
Ground level platform
Portable Building Co. waiting room
Goods siding with standard gauge section
Nameboard and seat

Ecton for Warslow
Ground level platform
Portable Building Co. waiting room
Loop and goods siding with standard gauge
  section
9-chain branch into Cheese Factory
Nameboard and seat

Hulme End
Ground level platform
'Large' Portable Building Co. station
  building with booking office
Run-round loop
Two goods sidings with standard gauge
  sections (holding approx. 12 wagons)
Locomotive shed with two sidings
Carriage shed with two sidings
Water tower
Weigh-bridge
Stores for cycles/parcels and beer
Permanent way stores
5-lever open ground frame
Wooden coaling stage for locomotives
Lifting gear for heavy repairs
Loading gauges (2)
Coal merchant's offices
Nameboard and seat

Note: There were originally 12 station seats, most of which were lettered to show the names of the stations at which they were positioned. There was, generally speaking, one of these seats at each station, Wetton Mill and Thor's Cave being important enough to warrant two seats each!

Appendix Three

Some Comparative Data Relating to Calthrop's System

The Calthrop system, with its strict limits on speed and axle loading, permitted a reduction in rail weight (and therefore cost). This factor is forcibly revealed by the following table, which shows at a glance the significant savings made possible by the application of Calthrop standards. It should be noted that some of the lines included in the table were 2 ft gauge routes using locomotives and rolling stock of much lighter construction than those working on the Leek & Manifold Railway.

Railway	Gauge	Rail Type	Weight per yd
Leek & Manifold	2 ft 6 in.	flat-bottom	35 lb.
Vale of Rheidol	2 ft 0 in.	flat-bottom	50 lb.
Cavan & Leitrim	3 ft 0 in.	flat-bottom	45 lb. (later 60–65 lb. f/b)
Lynton & Barnstaple	2 ft 0 in.	flat-bottom	40 lb.
Talyllyn Railway	2 ft 3 in.	flat-bottom	44 lb.
Cork Blackrock & Passage	3 ft 0 in.	double-headed	68½ lb.
Clogher Valley Railway	3 ft 0 in.	flat-bottom	45 lb. (later 50 or 55 lb. f/b)

Light rails notwithstanding, the Manifold coaches were larger than those on other narrow gauge lines. This is shown by the following table which compares L&MVLR passenger stock with modern vehicles from other railways.

Railway	Length between end bulkheads	Width
Leek & Manifold	42 ft 0 in.	8 ft (over roof)
Vale of Rheidol	32 ft 0 in.	6 ft
Cavan & Leitrim	40 ft 0 in.	7 ft
Lynton & Barnstaple	35 ft 2 in.	6 ft (over steps)
Cork Blackrock & Passage	36 ft 0 in.	7 ft

Further Reading

The Leek & Manifold Railway has received considerable attention from local historians, and those seeking further information should consult some of the following books or articles. Most of these titles are out of print, but journals such as *The Engineer* should be available in any university library. The short monograph by 'Manifold' can be recommended, while Basil Jeuda's well-researched monograph will be useful to readers hoping to obtain further information on the standard gauge line between Leek and Waterhouses.

Basil Jeuda. *The Leek, Caldon & Waterhouses Railway* (1980).
'Manifold'. *The Leek & Manifold Valley Light Railway* (1955).
R. Keys & L. Porter. *The Manifold Valley and its Light Railway* (1972).
Christopher P. Nicholson & Peter Barnes. *Railways in the Peak District* (1971).
Gilbert J. Stoker. The Leek & Manifold Valley Light Railway. *The Railway Magazine*, 1904.
Nellie Kirkham. *Ecton Mines*.
Basil Mercer. The Leek & Manifold Narrow Gauge Railway. *The Railway Magazine*, April 1917.
Charles F. Klapper. The Leek & Manifold Section of the LMSR. *The Railway Magazine*, October 1932.
H.C. Casserley. The Leek & Manifold Valley Light Railway. *The Railway Magazine*, September and October 1945.
D.M. Smith. The Closing of the Manifold Valley Light Railway. *The Railway Magazine*, May 1934.
R.E. Tustin. Leek & Manifold Valley Light Railway Compo Brake. *Model Railway Constructor*, April 1958.
R.E. Tustin. Leek & Manifold Valley Light Railway Third. *Model Railway Constructor*, August 1958.
R.E. Tustin. Leek & Manifold Valley Light Railway Locomotives. *Model Railway Constructor*, November 1956.
W.T.F. Castle. The Leek & Manifold Valley Light Railway (LMSR). *Model Railway News*, March 1931.

Index